Fighting for Honor

Japanese Americans and World War II

Michael L. Cooper

Clarion Books
New York

To my good friend
Mike Duniven

Clarion Books
a Houghton Mifflin Company imprint
215 Park Avenue South, New York, NY 10003
Copyright © 2000 by Michael L. Cooper

The text was set in 12-point Janson.

Book design by Richard Granald.

For information about permission
to reproduce selections from this book,
write to Permissions, Houghton Mifflin Company,
215 Park Avenue South, New York, NY 10003.

www.houghtonmifflinbooks.com

Printed in U.S.A.

Library of Congress Cataloging-in-Publication Data

Cooper, Michael L., 1950–
Fighting for honor : Japanese Americans and World War II / Michael L. Cooper.
p.   cm.
Includes bibliographical references.
Summary: Examines the history of Japanese in the United States, focusing on their treatment
during World War II, including the mass relocation to internment camps and the
distinguished service of Japanese Americans in the American military.
ISBN 0-395-91375-6
1. Japanese Americans—Evacuation and relocation, 1942–1945—Juvenile literature.
2. World War, 1939–1945—Japanese Americans—Juvenile literature.
[1. Japanese Americans—Evacuation and relocation, 1942–1945.
2. World War, 1939–1945—Japanese Americans.] I. Title.

D769.8.A6 C66 2000
940.53'089956—dc21
00-026855

RO 10 9 8 7 6 5 4 3 2 1

The principle on which this country was founded and by which it has always been governed is that Americanism is a matter of mind and heart; Americanism is not, and never was, a matter of race or ancestry. A good American is one who is loyal to this country and to our creed of liberty and democracy.

—PRESIDENT FRANKLIN D. ROOSEVELT

Contents

Acknowledgments

Special thanks to Cameron Trowbridge and the entire archival staff at the Japanese American National Museum, Los Angeles; to Jack Von Euw, Curator of the Pictorial Collection, The Bancroft Library, University of California, Berkeley; to Kara Paw-Pa, Collections Manager, National Japanese American Historical Society, San Francisco; and to Sharon Shelton, English teacher, Whitley County (Ky.) High School, for her helpful comments on the manuscript.

MAINE

VT.

N.H.

MASS.

CONN.

R.I.

NEW YORK

PENNSYLVANIA

N.J.

DEL.

MD.

MICHIGAN

SCONSIN

ILLINOIS

INDIANA

OHIO

W. VIRGINIA

VIRGINIA

URI

KENTUCKY

NSAS

TENNESSEE

N. CAROLINA

S. CAROLINA

er ◆

ne ◆

MISSISSIPPI

ALABAMA

GEORGIA

ANA

FLORIDA

War Relocation
Authority Camps

1

War Hysteria

"PEARL HARBOR. WE ARE AT WAR! The Japs bombed Hawaii and the entire fleet has been sunk. I just can't believe it. I don't know what in the hell is going to happen to us. . . ."

Charles Kikuchi, a student at the University of California, wrote these words in his diary on December 7, 1941, just hours after the early-morning surprise attack on the U.S. Navy and Army Air Force bases at Pearl Harbor. The devastating Japanese air raid killed thousands of sailors and soldiers and crippled America's entire naval fleet in the Pacific Ocean. It was the beginning of the war with Japan. Charles was afraid not only for his country, the United States, but also for his family and other people of Japanese heritage living in America.

Immediately after the bombing of Pearl Harbor, FBI agents raided the businesses and homes of U.S. residents of Japanese ancestry. They searched basements, attics, and closets, looking for hidden radio transmitters, maps, and other evidence of espionage.

"My dad was head of a couple of organizations which I guess the FBI considered dangerous or subversive. So one morning, about seven

1

The Japanese attack on Pearl Harbor shocked, frightened, and angered Americans.
LIBRARY OF CONGRESS

o'clock, they broke through our front door and came in with submachine guns," recalled George Akimoto, who was then a twenty-year-old college student in Stockton, California. "They questioned us, and then they said, 'We're going to have to take him.' They took my mother's knitting book that was written in Japanese—you know, knit one, purl two. They thought it was a code book. That was the only evidence they took when they took my old man. . . . So they took him and put him in the local jail. This was in the wintertime. He didn't even take his topcoat because he thought he would be back in a day or two. Next thing we know, we got a letter from Bismarck, North Dakota. He's up there in a camp freezing his butt off in the snow up there without his topcoat!"

The agents found no suggestion of spying in any of the homes they searched. Nevertheless, they arrested seven thousand individuals, including Buddhist priests, community leaders, and Japanese-language teachers. The government said these people might be dangerous spies or saboteurs and sent them to faraway prisons. Although most of the people arrested had lived in this country for twenty, thirty, or more years, they were not American citizens. U.S. law at that time did not allow men and women born in Japan to become citizens.

"He had become a man without a country," recalled Jeanne Wakatsuki Houston, who was seven years old when the FBI came to her home near Santa Monica, California, and took away her father. The federal agents sent Mr. Wakatsuki to Bismarck, where he was imprisoned with hundreds of other Japanese aliens. "The land of his birth was at war with America; yet after thirty-five years here he was still prevented by law from becoming an American citizen. He was suddenly a man with no rights who looked exactly like the enemy."

Fewer than one percent of the 130 million people in the United States in the early 1940s were of Japanese ancestry. Nearly all of them—112,353 people—lived in Washington, Oregon, and California. They included 40,869 Japanese citizens who had immigrated to America years earlier. These people were commonly referred to as Issei, a Japanese word that means "first generation." The remaining 71,484 were the children of these immigrants. Because they had been born in the United States, they were citizens. They were called Nisei, a Japanese word that means "second generation." The destructive attack on Pearl Harbor and the resulting war led to open persecution of the small Japanese minority, citizens and noncitizens alike.

On December 8, 1941, Congress declared war on Japan. In September 1940, Japan, Italy, and Germany had signed the Tripartite Pact, which pledged the three countries to defend one another. So Germany and Italy, which had been at war for two years against France and Great Britain, immediately declared war against the United States. The nation was plunged into World War II, the biggest conflict mankind had ever known.

The Japanese Imperial Army quickly followed its victory at Pearl Harbor with other military victories. It captured Wake Island, the British colony of Hong Kong, and the U.S. territories of Guam and the Philippine Islands. Japanese soldiers even invaded Alaska's remote Aleutian Islands. Alaska, like Hawaii at the time, was not a state but a U.S. territory. Many Americans feared that the aggressive enemy was marching from island to island straight across the Pacific Ocean— straight toward the West Coast. Los Angeles or San Francisco, they feared, might become a second Pearl Harbor.

Los Angeles residents thought they were being invaded one day in February 1942 when a Japanese submarine surfaced near the coast north of the city and fired several shots from its single cannon at an oil refinery. Residents were startled the following night by the screams of air-raid sirens and by the *pop-pop-pop* of anti-aircraft fire. "Madness was loosed," reported the *Los Angeles Times*. "The city was blacked out. Searchlights stroked the sky. Anti-aircraft guns opened up. The night was laced with tracers and explosives."

The submarine did little damage to the refinery, and the air raid had been a false alarm, but both incidents made people so fearful that they turned against the local Japanese.

"Dirty yellow-belly Japs," fumed an angry Caucasian. "Sneaky backstabbing son of a bitches." Americans cursed the Japanese as no enemy of the United States had ever been cursed. Soon government propaganda was depicting them as rats, dogs, gorillas, and snakes. Newspapers constantly published hate-filled articles. "Let us have no patience with the enemy or with anyone whose veins carry his blood,"

Propaganda heightened the public's suspicion and hatred of people of Japanese ancestry.

wrote Henry McLemore, a popular columnist. "Personally, I hate the Japanese. And that goes for all of them."

Caucasians suspected Issei fishermen of spying on Navy ships, and farmers of plotting to blow up bridges or poison water supplies. Many people thought all Japanese were the enemy. "A Jap's a Jap. They are a dangerous element," declared John L. DeWitt, an Army general in charge of wartime security on the West Coast. "There is no way to determine their loyalty. . . . It makes no difference whether he is an American citizen; theoretically he is still a Japanese and you can't change him."

The government imposed curfews and restrictions on all "enemy aliens." These people—Germans, Italians, and Japanese—were citizens of the nations at war against the United States. They were not allowed to go near docks, airports, dams, power plants, or military bases. They had to be in their homes between 9:00 P.M. and 6:00 A.M. During the day they were only allowed to go to work and to travel no farther than five miles from their homes.

Such restrictions fell hardest on the Japanese, because they were clearly distinguishable from Caucasians. Italian and German aliens, on the other hand, looked like most Caucasian Americans, so they were able to move about without raising suspicion. The restrictions were in practice difficult for all Asians, because whites could not differentiate among the various nationalities. Chinese, trying to escape harassment, wore buttons reading, I'M CHINESE. Some even added, I HATE THE JAPS AS MUCH AS YOU DO.

General DeWitt declared Terminal Island, off Los Angeles, where two thousand Japanese lived, a restricted area because Long Beach Naval Shipyard occupied part of the island. FBI agents swept across the island, arresting 336 men. A few weeks later, the Army ordered the

Franklin D. Roosevelt signing the declaration of war against Japan. NATIONAL ARCHIVES

remaining residents—mostly women, children, and the elderly—to evacuate their homes within forty-eight hours and move inland. The Army issued similar orders to the Japanese community on Bainbridge Island, Washington, across Puget Sound from Seattle's busy harbor. These evacuations were just the beginning; a much larger one would soon follow.

In February 1942, President Franklin D. Roosevelt signed Executive Order 9066, a broad law giving the Army power to establish restricted military areas and to forcibly remove from their homes people living in those areas. Initially, the government told Japanese residents to simply take their families inland, away from Military Area No. 1. This restricted zone covered the western halves of California and Oregon, the southern half of Arizona, and the western two thirds of Washington State. Hundreds of people did move eastward. But the first groups that relocated to the neighboring states of Idaho, Nevada, and northern Arizona met so much hostility from local white people that this plan had to be abandoned. "The Japs live like rats, breed like rats and act like rats," Chase Clark, Idaho's governor, declared in a speech. "We don't want them buying or leasing land or becoming permanently located in our state." So the U.S. government adopted a more drastic solution.

President Roosevelt established the War Relocation Authority (WRA) on March 18, 1942. Its purpose was to set up and administer relocation camps for all people of Japanese heritage living on the West Coast.

Soldiers tacked up posters in dozens of Japanese American communities, notifying residents they would be evacuated. "I remember those posters, all of a sudden on every telephone pole," recalled Ben Tateishi, who was eleven years old at the time. "The posters made us feel guilty and that we better stick together. We were just fearful. And the same question occurred to [each of] us: 'What's going to happen to us?'"

The posters instructed all residents to close their businesses, withdraw from school, board their dogs and cats, and quickly make all other necessary preparations to leave their homes within a few days. The evacuation orders applied to rich and poor, old and young—businessmen, lawyers, doctors, nurses, teachers, housewives, farmers, fishermen, high school students, grade school children, and babies. The

The Army began the evacuation three months after the war began.
LIBRARY OF CONGRESS

authorities even removed boys and girls of Japanese ancestry from orphanages.

Issei- and Nisei-owned pharmacies, hardware stores, and grocery stores in Japanese neighborhoods hastily held going-out-of-business sales, selling their merchandise at bargain prices. "Secondhand dealers descended like wolves to prey on the helpless," reported one man.

"Women cried awfully. Some of them smashed their stuff, broke it up right before the buyers' eyes because they offered such ridiculous prices."

In farm country the "land vultures" swooped down, offering extremely low prices to the desperate Issei. A Compton, California, Issei farmer sold his horse, three tons of hay, three quarters of a ton of fertilizer, a harrow, a cultivator, and a plow—all of which had cost him several thousand dollars—for only one hundred dollars.

Some evacuees stored furniture and clothing in local churches. Other people simply locked their homes and hoped everything would be there if and when they returned. The Issei entrusted an estimated $200 million worth of property to lawyers and to Caucasian friends.

Each person took only what clothing he or she could carry in a couple of suitcases or boxes. Then they gathered at bus stations, train depots, or street corners to wait for the soldiers. WRA authorities informed the evacuees that they were being sent to remote camps to live for the duration of the war. Although they were told to prepare for a pioneer life, none of them knew what lay ahead.

"I remember walking down the street to the assembly point," said Tateishi, "and I remember seeing our neighbors peeking out of their curtains. They were friends we used to go to school with, and yet they were not coming out and saying, 'Gee, I'm sorry you're leaving,' 'Wish you luck,' 'Come back,' or whatever. They were afraid of being accused of being Jap lovers. Anyway, I felt like an outcast walking down that street. We had a strong feeling of shame. We felt we were going to be taken away as if we did something wrong."

It was very frightening, another boy recalled, when he and his neighbors were on the bus. "The soldiers came aboard and all had their guns. The window shades were drawn. We didn't know where we were

Residents of Bainbridge Island, Washington, were among the first people forced to leave their homes.
LIBRARY OF CONGRESS

Within just a few weeks, soldiers had removed everyone of Japanese heritage from the three Pacific Coast states.
LIBRARY OF CONGRESS

Nearly two thirds of the people evacuated, like these brothers, were American citizens.
NATIONAL ARCHIVES

going. It was just a horrible feeling because we didn't know what was happening to us."

Within a few weeks, from California to Washington State, tens of thousands of people had been taken from their homes. The authorities sent them to sixteen fairgrounds and racetracks being used as assembly centers. All but three of these facilities were in California. The WRA officials housed everyone in horse stalls and hastily constructed tarpaper barracks. One man described the assembly center where his family was sent: "At that time I was a junior in high school in Auburn [Washington], and I certainly didn't feel that my brother, my sisters, or I would be evacuated," said John Kanda, who lived south of Seattle. But

"In March 1942, we were sent to Pinedale Assembly Camp, which is right outside Fresno, California.

"Pinedale was a camp like all camps, surrounded by barbed wire, and inside there was a sentry line which you're not supposed to pass. There wasn't a blade of grass in that place or a tree. It was just sand and dust and the tar-paper barracks, and it was really hot. I can recall everything the neighbors said; they were talking on either side of you, and it was just like you were right next to them. There was no privacy. You could even hear people whisper; it was just dreadful."

The Issei and Nisei stayed in the temporary assembly centers for several weeks while the WRA hastily built large relocation camps in faraway sections of the country.

"I was very sad," Kanda said. "I thought it couldn't be happening; and believing what was in the textbooks and all on government and the Constitution, I just said, hey, this can't be happening to us. But it was."

The internment of Japanese aliens and their American children during World War II was the largest single forced evacuation in American history. It was a unique and tragic episode. Why did it happen?

2

Asians in America

MANY IMMIGRANTS to the United States have been met with hostility, but the hostility was worse for Japanese and other Asians.

The Chinese, the first Asians to migrate in large numbers to America, came during the California gold rush. Young men from the province of Canton appeared in the Sacramento Valley gold fields in 1849. About the same time, Chinese entrepreneurs opened restaurants, laundries, and grocery stores in the booming port of San Francisco, establishing America's first Chinatown.

After the Civil War, when millions of Europeans began immigrating to the United States, Chinese laborers helped build the first transcontinental railroad, which was completed in 1869 and was important in opening the West to settlement by white people.

Although Caucasians valued the Chinese as cheap, docile, and hard-working laborers, they were also extremely prejudiced against them. People openly called the Chinese "chinks," "coolies," and "slant eyes." Whites, mindful of China's teeming population, worried loudly

The Chinese were the first Asians to immigrate to America. This is a street scene from San Francisco's Chinatown in the late nineteenth century. LIBRARY OF CONGRESS

that "Asiatic hordes" would overrun the country. In several western towns, white mobs attacked Chinese people. One of the worst incidents occurred in Los Angeles in 1871, when rampaging whites lynched twenty Chinese. There was so much prejudice that in 1882, when fewer than 100,000 Chinese people lived in the United States, Congress passed the Chinese Exclusion Act, which made emigration from China to the United States illegal.

At the time, Americans were unconcerned about Japanese immi-grants, because only a few hundred had come to the United States. Japan, a small island nation on the other side of the world, had been an isolated feudal society for 250 years. The country's rulers did not allow their subjects to leave, nor did they allow westerners to visit. Commodore Matthew C. Perry's famous voyage to Japan in 1853 marked the end of the nation's isolation. Three decades later, the gov-ernment began to allow its citizens to go abroad.

Jeanne Wakatsuki's father was typical of the first Japanese who immigrated to America. Wakatsuki Ko was born in the small town of Ka-ke near Hiroshima. He left Japan in 1904 at the age of seventeen. He traveled first to Hawaii, where he met a lawyer who offered him a job as a houseboy at his home in Idaho. Wakatsuki Ko worked for the lawyer's family for five years before meeting the woman who became his wife at a farmers' market in Spokane. He then worked at various jobs—cook, lumberjack, farmer, and finally fisherman, operating two boats from Terminal Island.

Young Japanese men like Wakatsuki Ko sailed across the Pacific Ocean to America in the late nineteenth and early twentieth centuries for the same reasons millions of other people migrated to the New World. They came to find jobs and the opportunity to build comfort-able lives for themselves. There was no better class of laborers, stated one Caucasian, than the Japanese. They toiled beside Mexicans, Filipinos, and Chinese in canneries and mines, on farms and fishing boats.

Minour Yasui described his family's journey to America and the hard work and discrimination they faced. "My paternal grandfather, Shinataro Yasui, had come out of the rice fields of rural Okayama, during the mid-1890s, to work on the railroads in Idaho, Montana,

Washington, and Oregon. Having put aside some money from his earnings as a railroad-gang laborer, he later sent for his two older sons (my paternal uncles), who came to the U.S. before 1900, also to work on the railroads. . . . My father, Masuo Yasui, came to the U.S. in 1903, at age sixteen. Because he was so slight that he could not physically perform the hard labor on the railroad gangs, he became a 'schoolboy' in Portland, Oregon, doing domestic work, learning to cook, laundering clothes, and working in the garden. He wanted to become a lawyer, but found out soon enough that the legal profession was barred to him because of his Japanese alienage. He also discovered that he could not become a U.S. citizen because he was an Oriental."

In the last two decades of the nineteenth century, the number of Japanese in the United States jumped from just a few hundred to some fifty thousand. Nearly all of them were young men. They lived and traveled together, working at various jobs until they were ready to marry.

Japanese men outnumbered Japanese women in the United States one hundred to one. They could not marry women of other races because of state laws prohibiting interracial marriage. Few immigrants could afford to return to Japan to search for wives, so men like Minour Yasui's father asked relatives back home to locate suitable mates. Their brothers or fathers sent them photographs of prospective wives, who were dubbed "picture brides." When a match was made, the woman sailed to the United States to meet her husband for the first time. Anyone born on American soil could be a citizen, so their children, the Nisei, were American citizens. But the Nisei were not treated like other citizens.

The same kind of xenophobia, or fear and hatred of foreigners, that affected the Chinese beset the Japanese. They were "different in color; different in ideals; different in race; different in ambitions; different in their theory of political economy and government," in the words of one white man. "They speak a different language; they worship a different God; they have not in common with the Caucasian a single trait." Such attitudes created numerous problems for the Issei and their children.

The San Francisco school board caused an international incident in 1906 when it ordered the ninety-three boys and girls of Japanese descent in the public schools to attend the city's Chinese school. The order angered people in faraway Japan.

The proud Japanese did not want to be grouped with the poor masses from neighboring China. They also were angry because their nation had a sophisticated culture two thousand years older than that of the United States. And just a few decades after Commodore Perry's trip, the Japanese government had created a prosperous economy as well as a large, modern navy and army. The small nation had undergone a remarkable transformation from a land of fishermen and farmers into one of the world's most powerful industrial nations. The Japanese people resented ignorant Americans and Europeans who treated them as inferior. Japanese officials complained about the San Francisco insult to President Theodore Roosevelt.

The president respected the traditional culture of Japan as well as the country's growing industrial and military power. He summoned San Francisco's mayor and school board officials to Washington and persuaded them not to make Nisei students attend a segregated school. In return, the Japanese government agreed to restrict immigration to America. This informal understanding became known as the Gentlemen's Agreement.

Seven years after the school controversy in San Francisco, the

California state legislature passed the Alien Land Law, which prohibited people who were not U.S. citizens from owning property in the state. And in 1924, Congress passed the Johnson-Reed Act, which favored emigration by people from northern Europe while practically stopping emigration from Africa, South America, and Asia. These state and federal laws reflected a growing xenophobia across the nation. Many people blamed foreign newcomers for the nation's mounting urban problems, such as slums, poverty, and crime. Some historians believe the resentment over these exclusionary laws contributed to the Japanese decision seventeen years later to attack the United States at Pearl Harbor.

By the time Congress passed the Johnson-Reed Act, there were nearly 100,000 Japanese people in the United States. Nearly all of them lived in the three Pacific Coast states. For many years, most of these immigrants had labored at menial jobs and lived simply. They pooled their money to create *tanomoshi* or cooperative banks from which members could borrow to invest in homes, farms, and businesses.

The immigrants had to be resourceful in other ways, too, such as getting around laws against owning land. Shig Doi was a Nisei who lived with his parents on an eighty-five-acre farm in Auburn, California, northeast of Sacramento, the state capital. The land had been purchased in Doi's older brother's name. As a citizen, the boy could legally own property. California Issei frequently circumvented the state's law against aliens owning property by buying homes and farms in their children's names.

Despite the barriers, many Japanese immigrants became comfortably middle class. A few even realized the American dream of becoming millionaires.

George Shima migrated to America in 1889 and first worked as a common laborer. He saved his earnings and began buying marshland along the San Joaquin River. Most people thought the property was unfit for farming, but Shima drained the marsh and planted potatoes. The land proved very fertile, and Shima soon had a thriving farm and a new nickname, the Potato King. He eventually amassed 28,000 acres of land worth millions of dollars in the San Joaquin Valley.

Most Japanese men and women worked in farming, either growing crops or selling them. One government official noted that the Japanese were an important part of the huge agricultural industry for which California had become so famous. "Their thrift is remarkable, their patience inexhaustible," he said, "and they are natural gardeners, seem-

Many Japanese immigrants, such as these men and women picking lettuce on a California farm, worked in agriculture. LIBRARY OF CONGRESS

The Shibuyas, who are standing behind their six children, immigrated to America in 1904 with only sixty dollars. They created a prosperous business growing chrysanthemums, built a nice home, and sent their children to good universities. The Army sent the family to a WRA camp in the spring of 1942. NATIONAL ARCHIVES

ing to read the secrets of the very soil. . . ." Caucasians, if they knew any Japanese at all, knew them as vendors of celery, cucumbers, lettuce, apples, and strawberries at local farmers' markets.

While many immigrants settled in farming communities, some preferred life in the big West Coast cities of Seattle, San Francisco, and Los Angeles. By the 1920s, one fourth of America's entire Japanese population lived in or near Los Angeles. Downtown, along East First and San Pedro Streets, was Little Tokyo, the country's largest Japanese neighborhood. It consisted of several blocks of restaurants, hotels, shops, department stores, and theaters that showed Japanese movies.

Late in the 1930s, the neighborhood organized an annual Nisei Week Festival, proudly displaying the first generation of Japanese Americans. Thousands of Caucasians visited Little Tokyo during Nisei Week to watch the parade, admire the beauty pageant contestants, and eat lots of sushi, soba noodles, and rice cakes.

By the end of the 1930s, most Issei had been in America for several decades. They had come to this country with little other than a willingness to work hard. They had saved their money, established thriving businesses, and created comfortable homes. Despite their success, they still faced much hostility.

It was an age of prejudice in America with discrimination against Jews, Mexicans, African Americans, and Asians of all nationalities. These people were barred from many neighborhoods and jobs. Restaurants, hotels, swimming pools, and barber and beauty shops refused to serve black, Hispanic, and Asian customers.

"Even the teachers were that way in the high school," Shig Doi said, recalling the prejudice he felt as a teenager. "There was a certain feeling—the white kids used to kind of keep to themselves, and we used to keep to ourselves. At certain times, some of us would mix with the whites, but as a whole, we kept to ourselves."

It was an awkward time for Nisei teenagers. They could not date Caucasians. White classmates did not invite them to their homes. And Nisei boys were too small to play popular sports such as football or basketball. When several Nisei at one school proved to be good baseball players, they were kept from playing by white parents who complained loudly to the coach that the "Japs" were taking over the team.

Adults were more prejudiced than their children. The students at Hollywood Junior High School elected John Fujio Aiso student body president, but parents protested so loudly that the principal abolished all student government until Aiso graduated. Three years later, while a senior at Hollywood High School, Aiso won an oratory contest sponsored by the American Legion. Officials would not allow the Nisei boy to represent his school at the national competition in Washington, D.C. Instead, they sent a white classmate, who won the contest with his speech on the American Constitution.

The Nisei were awkwardly caught between their parents and their peers. They wanted to be like other young Americans, but their Issei parents wanted them to appreciate their heritage.

"My father taught me *shuushin,* the Japanese code of ethics," said Togo Tanaka, a Nisei born in California, "and he instilled in me the values of honor, loyalty, service, and obligation that had been taught to him by his forebears in Japan." The first generation of Japanese Americans, like Togo, combined two sets of traditions.

"My home life was a queer mixture of the Occident and the Orient," another boy recalled. "I sat down to American breakfasts and Japanese lunches. . . . I became equally adept with knife and fork and with chopsticks. . . . I hung my stocking over the fireplace at Christmas and toasted *mochi* [a rice dish traditionally served on New Year's] at Japanese New Year. . . . I was spoken to by both parents in Japanese or in English. I answered in whichever was convenient or in a curious mixture of both."

Issei parents enrolled their children in special schools to learn the Japanese language and traditional customs. Wealthy parents sent their sons back to Japan to attend school; Nisei educated in Japan were called kibei. Most Issei enrolled their children in local Japanese-language schools.

Young people did not like attending two additional hours of school each afternoon when they could be outside playing ball or at the library doing their "real" class work. "It's not Japan here," one woman remembered complaining as a little girl. "It's America. So why should we have

This Dorothea Lange photograph shows schoolchildren from diverse ethnic backgrounds at the Raphael Weill Public School in San Francisco.
NATIONAL ARCHIVES

to learn and follow these stiff rules of behavior if we don't want to go back to Japan?"

The Issei valued education and encouraged their children to be good students. "Continue with American higher education," one father urged his sons. "Show the Americans your ability. That is your duty to your parents." Many Nisei obeyed. There were fewer than two hundred Japanese American students among the thousands of Caucasian students attending Seattle's nine high schools in 1937, but in that year's graduating classes three Nisei were valedictorians and two were salutatorians.

Despite their parents' emphasis on traditional Japanese values, the Nisei wanted to fit in with their classmates. Some changed their first names. A boy named Makoto became Mac, and another boy, named Shoji, became George. Or they simply chose popular names they liked such as John or James, Mary or Susan. These names had the added advantage of being easier than their given names for non-Japanese to pronounce.

Caucasians looked at the Nisei and saw Japanese, but the Nisei saw themselves differently. "I considered myself American, definitely. I didn't know Japan. It's true when I was four years old, my parents took us to Japan for about six months and left my two oldest brothers there [to attend school]. I have some memories of that, almost like a dream. But other than that I didn't know how to speak Japanese except to my parents in broken Japanese. We were going to Japanese school after our regular classes, but that was more because we had to, and I didn't personally feel I was part of Japan."

Nisei boys and girls grew up like most other American children. They went to school, watched the latest movies, and dreamed similar dreams. Many Nisei attended college despite widespread prejudice that barred them from most jobs. One doctor who attended medical school at the University of California at Berkeley said his class included Japanese, Chinese, and Jewish students, all of whom would have trouble finding medical jobs because of their heritage.

"The Japanese people finally have the money to send their kids to college," said Gene Sogioka, who was a young man in California at the time of evacuation. "But when you get out of college . . . there's no job. . . . They will not hire Japanese. So we end up working in the fruit markets or something like that."

The Nisei tried to overcome the prejudice that kept them out of the mainstream of American life. They organized Boy Scout and Girl Scout troops. The older Nisei joined Japanese American chapters of the Young Republicans and Young Democrats. One of the most active

Some Japanese Americans, such as the merchant in this famous Dorothea Lange photograph, protested against being treated like enemy aliens. NATIONAL ARCHIVES

associations was the Japanese American Citizens League (JACL). The Nisei joined the JACL hoping to change laws that discriminated against people of Japanese heritage.

"I'm proud I'm an American citizen of Japanese ancestry," declared a JACL creed adopted in 1940. "I pledge myself to do honor to her [America] at all times and places; to defend her against all enemies, foreign and domestic; to actively assume my duties and obligations as a citizen, cheerfully and without any reservation whatsoever, in the hope that I may become a better American in a greater America."

At the time the JACL adopted this creed, many Americans anticipated war with Japan, but few thought the U.S. government would imprison tens of thousands of citizens and noncitizens alike.

"Some of the younger kids around town get angry at us because they say, 'Why didn't you protest?' like people do now," explained

George Akimoto. "They don't know what they're talking about. In those days, you just didn't do things that way. Actually we just didn't have the time; it was a shock and you didn't have the time to sit down and think about it. You just do what you're told and try to make the best of it."

The Issei and Nisei were bitter about being sent to the internment camps. Although photographs of them often show smiling faces, their diaries and letters show another side. Some cursed America and prayed for Japan to win the war. Others wanted to prove that they were loyal citizens, that the mistrust was unfounded and unfair. The war presented the Nisei with a huge challenge. How they met that challenge would affect Americans of Japanese ancestry for generations to come.

Large numbers of armed soldiers oversaw the evacuation. NATIONAL ARCHIVES

3

Barbed Wire Communities

Snow upon the rooftop
Snow upon the coal
Winter in Wyoming
Winter in my soul

—Miyuki Aoyama, *Heart Mountain Sentinel*

By the first anniversary of the Pearl Harbor attack, every man, woman, and child of Japanese descent on the West Coast—over 110,000 people—had been imprisoned in a WRA camp.

They were disheartened by their new surroundings. "After living in well-furnished homes with every modern convenience, suddenly being forced to live the life of a dog is something which one cannot so readily forget," one man remarked. "Down in our hearts we cried and cursed this government. . . ." Despite such bitter feelings, many of the Issei and Nisei wanted to prove they were trustworthy citizens.

Several hundred people, hoping to demonstrate their loyalty and to escape harassment, volunteered to move to Manzanar in March of

Dorothea Lange's photograph of Manzanar during a sandstorm. NATIONAL ARCHIVES

1942, several months before the camp was finished. Manzanar, located in the Owens Valley 225 miles northeast of Los Angeles, was a starkly beautiful site not far from the lowest and driest spot in America, Death Valley. The volunteers helped build dozens of wood-and-tarpaper buildings to house some ten thousand people.

That spring and summer the WRA constructed nine other camps, all but two in the Far West. The second camp in California was Tule

Ansel Adams's photograph captures the lonely isolation of the camps.
NATIONAL ARCHIVES

Lake, near Oregon. There were two camps, Poston and Gila River, in Arizona. There was Minidoka in Idaho, Heart Mountain in Wyoming, Topaz in Utah, and Amache in Colorado. The two WRA camps farthest from the West Coast were Rohwer and Jerome, both in Arkansas. The government called these camps "wartime communities" and the people confined in them "residents," "colonists," or "evacuees."

All the WRA camps were built in remote parts of the country, where few people would choose to live. Tule Lake, high in the mountains of northern California, sounded pretty, but it was a dried-up, dusty lake bed. There were no trees. Winter temperatures at the camp, which was four thousand feet above sea level, dropped to minus 25 degrees Fahrenheit. Amache was located on the dry plains of southeast Colorado, where prairie dogs and rattlesnakes outnumbered people. These creatures, camp residents suspected, were friendlier than the inhabitants of the nearest town, Lamar, who posted signs reading, JAPS NOT WANTED. Jerome, in Arkansas, was surrounded by a swamp full of poisonous water moccasins and copperheads.

Air conditioning was not widely used at the time, and the summer heat at the camps was nearly unbearable. At Poston, where eighteen thousand people were imprisoned, the August temperatures rose as high as 130 degrees Fahrenheit. "This scorching Hell," one man complained, "is a place beyond description and beyond belief." While the camp was divided into three separate communities officially called Poston I, Poston II, and Poston III, residents jokingly called them Poston, Toastin', and Roastin'. Sandstorms were another problem. They lasted several days, blowing gritty sand into the poorly constructed barracks and into clothing, beds, and even food.

Several hundred Caucasians managed each WRA facility. They included squads of 100 to 150 soldiers who stood guard day and night. While no one ever tried to escape, the guards sometimes had to break up fights or protests.

Each camp consisted of hundreds of nearly identical buildings lined up in neat rows. The rows were divided into blocks of fourteen barracks each, along with a dining hall, a recreation hall, men's and women's latrines, and a common shower room. A single wood-and-tarpaper barracks housed 250 to 300 persons. WRA officials planned for a family of four to live in each room, which was twenty feet wide and twenty-five feet long. But extended families pleaded to stay together, and as many as ten people crowded into a single room. The Spartan structures were similar to the temporary barracks being built on Army bases to house hundreds of thousands of new soldiers training for the war. The barracks had no closets, shelves, or furniture of any kind other than cots and oil-burning stoves for heat.

The residents set to work making their bleak quarters more comfortable. The men gathered scrap lumber to build tables and chairs, while the women sewed curtains and made pillows. These improvements helped, but the rooms were still uninviting.

"The cubicles we had were too small for anything you might call 'living,'" recalled Jeanne Wakatsuki, whose family was moved to

A squad of soldiers stood guard at each WRA camp. NATIONAL ARCHIVES

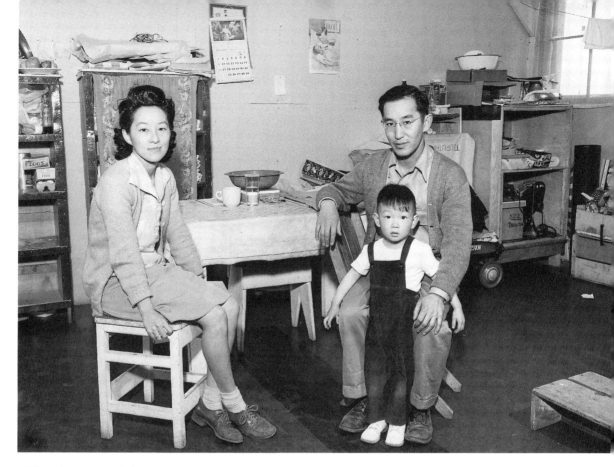

A family in one of their small rooms. LIBRARY OF CONGRESS

Manzanar in April 1942. Her father remained imprisoned in Bismarck. Twelve of them—brothers, sisters, brother-in-law, mother, and grandmother—lived in two rooms. "Mama couldn't cook meals there. It was impossible to find any privacy there. We slept there and spent most of our waking hours elsewhere."

One of the big problems at every camp was the lack of privacy. People shared latrines and showers. The latrine was an open room with twelve toilet bowls arranged two by two, back to back with no partitions. "My mother was a private person," Jeanne remembered, "and this was going to be agony for her, sitting down in public, among strangers."

Within weeks, the men had built screens for the latrines and made

Living conditions at the camps were crowded. NATIONAL ARCHIVES

many other improvements. The camps began to develop some of the regular routines common to many American communities. In the fall, just like boys and girls everywhere, nearly thirty thousand Nisei children had to start school. The WRA set up makeshift classrooms, but the camp schools were not very good.

"There was absolutely no equipment—especially for laboratory courses—and there was really a shortage beyond comprehension of textbooks. I never saw a Bunsen burner or a beaker or a flask until I got to college," complained a man who graduated from the high school at Tule Lake. "Every student in the camp school system suffered a great deal. I think they tried hard, but the equipment wasn't there, and the school was in a barracks. They had a blackboard and chalk and that was about it."

While the children were in school, the adults worked at a variety of jobs. The Manzanar farmers tended nearby orchards. The surrounding Owens Valley had once been an apple- and pear-growing region, but the orchards had been abandoned because of a water shortage. The camp residents built an irrigation system and pruned the trees. By the fall of 1942, they were harvesting bushel baskets full of shiny apples and pears.

Manzanar's farmers cultivated fifteen hundred acres of corn,

The first schools were short of teachers, books, and classrooms. NATIONAL ARCHIVES

Sports were important diversions. NATIONAL ARCHIVES

turnips, cucumbers, and other vegetables for their camp kitchens. They raised pigs, chickens, and cattle. The residents even made traditional Japanese foods such as tofu and soy sauce. The farmers also grew guayule, a plant that contains rubber. There was a nationwide shortage of rubber, which was needed to make millions of tires for the new trucks, jeeps, and airplanes being manufactured for the war.

Other camp residents made big camouflage nets that the Army used to hide military equipment on the battlefield. Many residents worked in the kitchens, laundries, or administrative offices. There were plenty of jobs for everyone.

Employees deposited their earnings of fifteen to twenty dollars a month into camp banks or spent it at camp stores. Merchants at

Manzanar solicited five dollars from each resident and bought clothing, food, furniture, and other merchandise to stock a big co-op store. The co-op soon employed over two hundred people and sold more than one million dollars in goods a year. The doctors, nurses, and dentists imprisoned in the camps staffed small hospitals to provide medical care for the other residents. People also established churches, post offices, fire departments, and newspapers. For recreation, the Issei gardened and made traditional Japanese crafts, while the Nisei played basketball, football, and baseball.

In many outward respects, the camps looked calm and fairly ordinary. But people were very unhappy. "The life here cannot be expressed," wrote Shizuko Horiuchi in a letter to a Caucasian friend. "Sometimes we are resigned to it, but when we see the barbed wire fences and the sentry tower with floodlights, it gives us a feeling of being prisoners in a 'concentration camp.' We try to be happy and yet, oftentimes, a gloominess does creep in. When I see the 'I am an American' editorials and write-ups, the 'equality of race' etc.—it seems to be mocking us in our faces."

Residents, angry at being imprisoned, often started heated arguments, fights, and riots. Gangs with names like Black Dragon Society, White Terror, and Blood Brothers declared themselves prisoners of war and staged protests. When soldiers at Poston detained two men for beating a third man whom they called *inu*, a severe Japanese insult meaning "dog" or "collaborator," hundreds of kitchen workers went on strike and marched through the camp, waving homemade Japanese flags. In December 1942, a crowd gathered outside Manzanar's administration building to demand the release of a prisoner arrested for beating another man. Soldiers fired into the crowd, killing three young men and wounding ten others.

Tule Lake was the most troublesome facility. When a violent riot broke out in November 1942, Army tanks rolled into the camp to stop the disturbance. The unrest became worse the following summer, after the government transferred twelve thousand anti-American protestors to Tule Lake. The northern California camp, more than any of the other WRA facilities, resembled a prison. The Army kept six tanks and a whole battalion of soldiers there. High rows of barbed wire surrounded the barracks, and bright spotlights mounted on guard towers swept across the grounds all night.

Tule Lake radicals were openly defiant. Hundreds of men joined Sokuku Kenkyu Seinen-dan (Young Men's Association for the Study of the Mother Country), while women joined a sister organization, Joshi-dan. They demanded to be sent to Japan, and prepared by going to lectures on Japanese culture, studying the Japanese language, and attending Buddhist ceremonies. Young men with shaved heads and wearing gray sweatshirts and headbands emblazoned with the rising sun, Japan's national symbol, marched outdoors early each morning to perform calisthenics punctuated by bugle calls and frequent shouts of *"Banzai,"* a traditional Japanese cheer and battle cry, for the emperor. These militants protested against flying the U.S. flag over the camp, playing American-style music on radios, and anything that was not pro-Japan.

While no facility was as militant as Tule Lake, there were angry disturbances at other camps. Many of these occurred in late 1942, when the WRA announced it would ask residents to fill out a form titled "Application for Leave Clearance." The form, WRA officials explained, would help administrators determine the residents' loyalty. People who gave acceptable answers would be allowed to leave the camps and move to Chicago, Philadelphia, and other cities farther east, where there were fewer prejudices against the Japanese as well as plenty of war-industry jobs.

At the same time, the War Department wanted to identify men who could be trusted as combat soldiers. The Army planned to ask for Nisei volunteers to serve with the 442nd Regimental Team. President Roosevelt, acting in the president's role of commander in chief of the armed forces, announced the formation of this special battalion on February 1, 1943. In his short speech, Roosevelt gave a good definition of who was an American. "The principle on which this country was founded and by which it has always been governed is that Americanism is a matter of mind and heart; Americanism is not, and never was, a matter of race or ancestry. A good American is one who is loyal to this country and to our creed of liberty and democracy."

To prove they were good Americans, the Nisei first had to give the right answers on the "Application for Leave Clearance." The last two questions, numbers 27 and 28, caused a lot of unexpected trouble.

Question number 27 asked: "Are you willing to serve in the Armed Forces of the United States, in combat duty, wherever ordered?"

Camp residents objected to this question because they wondered why they should risk their lives in combat while their families were imprisoned and denied the rights the United States claimed to be fighting to protect. "I am going to say 'no' to anything as long as they treat me like an alien," declared one man. "When they treat me like a citizen, they can ask me questions that a citizen should answer."

The other troublesome question, number 28, asked: "Will you swear unqualified allegiance to the United States of America and faithfully defend the United States from any or all attack by foreign or domestic forces, and forswear any form of allegiance or obedience to the Japanese emperor or any other foreign government, power, or organization?"

If they answered yes, many Issei believed, they would become people without a country, renouncing their Japanese citizenship while not being allowed to become U.S. citizens. Questions 27 and 28 caused many heated arguments among camp residents.

Jack Nishida almost came to blows with his father over the questions. Jack supported the United States, but his father did not. "If Japan should lose the war," the elder Nishida threatened, "I'll take poison and die. Japan will never lose the war." Because of his parents, Jack became a "No-No boy," which was the slang expression for men who answered no to questions 27 and 28. "My folks felt that they were going to leave this country and go back to Japan. If that was the case, I was the only boy in the family so I had to go with them."

Tule Lake radicals campaigned vigorously from barracks to barracks, arguing against the loyalty questionnaire. People who said they wanted to answer the questionnaire were harassed and ostracized. Despite this, many camp residents filled out the "Application for Leave Clearance," answering yes to questions 27 and 28.

The answers encouraged the War Department. Recruiters visited each facility, urging men to enlist. There were 23,000 men of military age in the camps, and the Army hoped at least 3,600 of them would volunteer for the Nisei combat battalion. They would join several thousand Hawaiians of Japanese ancestry already in training. Initially only 1,256 men volunteered for the Army's special battalion.

Many Japanese Americans reacted angrily to the Army's recruitment efforts. "What do they take us for? Saps?" one man asked. "First, they changed my army status to 4C because of my ancestry, ran me out of town, and now they want me to volunteer for a suicide squad so I could get killed for this damned democracy."

And camp residents immediately began harassing the Army volunteers. "Those of us who volunteered were ostracized," one young man remembered. "There were catcalls and we got into fistfights. The kibei,

A young man at Amache signs up for the Army. NATIONAL ARCHIVES

those born in America but educated in Japan, threw food at us in the kitchen, and my poor mother, with three sons who had volunteered, was castigated mercilessly."

People called the volunteers *inu*, and children tagged along behind them, howling and barking. Their friends quit speaking to them. The Army volunteers received so many threats that they began walking in pairs for safety.

"We were really scorned by most people," recalled the mother of another young man who wanted to join the Army. "It was the most difficult thing which happened to us in our entire life. But we said to our son, 'We understand you. We want you to do whatever you feel is right. If you want to be a loyal citizen of the U.S.A. and be patriotic, we think it a very good thing.' So we gave our blessing and sent him out. . . . My son went to Italy and fought fierce battles, but he came home alive."

The men who defied their friends and neighbors to volunteer for the Army explained their reasons. "I joined because I always felt very strongly about patriotism," said Tom Kawaguchi, who had been at Topaz before joining the Nisei battalion. "I felt that this was my country. I didn't know any other country. When war broke out with Japan, I was ready to fight the enemy, and I had no qualms about whether it was Japanese or German or whatever. This was my country and I was ready to defend it."

Another man gave a simpler but more dramatic explanation. "The Army had said Nisei protestations of loyalty were so much hogwash. We had to have a demonstration in blood."

Jeanne Wakatsuki's father, who had attended a Japanese military school as a teenager, spoke to his son Woodrow about joining the Army. "When a soldier goes to war, he must go believing he is never coming back. That is why the Japanese are such courageous warriors. They are prepared to die. They expect nothing else. But to do that, you must believe in what you're fighting for. If you do not believe, you will not be willing to die. If you are not willing to die, you won't fight well."

Jeanne's brother Woody responded softly. "I will fight well, Papa. I am an American citizen. America is at war. The more of us who go into the Army, the sooner the war will be over, the sooner you and Mama will be out of here."

4

Training Camp

IN EARLY 1943, the Nisei recruits quietly left the internment camps and traveled to Camp Shelby near Hattiesburg in southern Mississippi for basic training. The young men were not the only Japanese Americans at that Army base. They met thirteen hundred Hawaiian soldiers of Japanese ancestry who made up the 100th Infantry Battalion. Their battalion motto was "Remember Pearl Harbor."

The Army planned to combine the mainlanders and the Hawaiians into one Japanese American battalion, which would be called the 442nd Regimental Combat Team. But first, the two groups had to learn to get along with one another.

The Hawaiian Islanders made fun of the Nisei, calling them kotonks. They said "kotonk" was the sound a coconut made when it dropped from the tree and hit the ground. And, the islanders joked, it was the sound the mainlanders' heads made hitting the floor during the many fights between the two groups.

The Hawaiians called themselves butaheads. *Buta* is Hawaiian for "pig." They were pigheaded. These men stubbornly defied Army dis-

Hawaiian volunteers for the Army. HAWAIIAN STATE ARCHIVES

cipline. The butaheads did not like having their hair cut, tying their shoes, or tucking their shirts into their trousers. They were proud of not being spit-and-polish soldiers.

The butaheads had their own language. They spoke a pidgin English, a unique combination of English, Hawaiian, and Japanese that only other people from Hawaii understood. For example, "You go stay go and I go stay come" translated meant "You keep going and I'll be coming after you."

The islanders were close-knit. Many of them had been in the National Guard together. And many had attended Honolulu's McKinley High School, which was nicknamed Tokyo High because it had so many Japanese American students. The 100th's Caucasian assistant commander, James Lovell, had been McKinley's vice-principal as well as its baseball and football coach.

Although the Hawaiians shared a common Japanese ancestry with the Nisei mainlanders, their recent pasts were different. Labor agents took the first Japanese men and women to the Hawaiian Islands in 1868 to work on sugar-cane plantations. Caucasians owned the vast plantations and controlled the island's government and economy. In 1900, Hawaii became a U.S. territory, and residents—the majority of whom were Filipino, Korean, Chinese, and Japanese—became American citizens. The largest single ethnic group in Hawaii at the beginning of World War II were the Japanese, who represented over one third of the island's population of 420,000. These people were not sent to relocation camps because they were a big part of Hawaii's labor force, and many worked on the American military bases.

Nonetheless, after the surprise attack on Pearl Harbor, the islands' other residents looked at the ethnic Japanese with suspicion and hatred. There were rumors that local Filipinos were sharpening their machetes to chop up their Japanese American neighbors in revenge for Japan's recent invasion of the Philippine Islands. The U.S. government imposed martial law on Hawaii as the FBI arrested hundreds of local Japanese Americans, who were angry at being thought disloyal. When the Army later asked for 3,500 volunteers from the islands, in a rush to prove their patriotism, 10,000 men crowded into the recruitment office.

The first group of soldiers left their island home in early June 1942 and sailed across the Pacific to the mainland United States. They had not been told when they would be leaving or where they were going. "Before we had any chance to bid goodby to our loved ones," one GI recalled, "we found ourselves on board a troopship sailing for God-knew-where. Speculation was rife that we were headed for a concentration camp."

Two weeks later the Hawaiians arrived at Camp McCoy, near Sparta in southwest Wisconsin. Their first assignment was to help build barracks, similar to those in the WRA camps, to accommodate thousands of new recruits coming to McCoy that fall for training. The Japanese American soldiers also stood guard at a nearby detention center, where German and Italian aliens, as well as 172 men from Hawaii, were being held. One soldier had the unusual task of guarding his imprisoned father.

In those first months, military officials carefully observed the 100th battalion to determine if these men would make good, loyal soldiers. Some commanders never learned to trust them. When President Roosevelt visited Fort Riley, Kansas, the military police kept two hundred Nisei troops under armed guard until the president departed. Other commanders thought Asian Americans were too small to be good fighters. The average Japanese American GI was only five feet four inches tall, weighed 125 pounds, and wore a shoe size of 3½.

Few people of Japanese heritage had ever served in the U.S. military. Before World War II, neither the Navy nor the Marines accepted them. The Army had drafted some five thousand young Nisei men in 1940 and 1941, but after Pearl Harbor, they were reassigned or discharged and sent to relocation camps. The Army reclassified Nisei of draft age as 4C, the category for aliens not subject to military service. But America needed every capable man to fight the war. So the Army proposed the all-Nisei battalion as a way to test the loyalty and ability of soldiers of Japanese heritage. The Nisei were eager to prove themselves.

Among the first people the friendly, outgoing Hawaiians won over were the residents of the farms and small towns around Camp McCoy. Few Wisconsinites—descendants of Scandinavian and German immigrants—had ever seen a Japanese American or any other kind of Asian. They invited the soldiers to picnics, dinners, and dances. When the soldiers' parents heard how well their sons were being treated on the mainland, they showed their appreciation by holding a big luau, or party, for two hundred Wisconsin servicemen stationed in Hawaii.

In spite of some opposition, Army commanders felt confident by the end of 1942 that Japanese Americans could be useful soldiers. They transferred the Hawaiian Islanders from McCoy south to Camp Shelby, where they would complete their combat training.

New recruits at Camp Shelby learn to use bayonets. NATIONAL ARCHIVES

Soldiers practice throwing grenades.
NATIONAL ARCHIVES

A machine gunner on maneuvers.
NATIONAL ARCHIVES

Nisei soldiers run across a portable pontoon bridge.
NATIONAL ARCHIVES

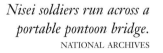

In some ways, Mississippi reminded the Hawaiians of their home. As in Hawaii, agriculture was the state's main industry and whites controlled everything. African Americans, who made up over half of the state's population, lived in shacks, and many worked as sharecroppers on white men's plantations. Few people of Asian heritage lived in Mississippi. In the late nineteenth century, plantation owners hired several hundred Chinese from the western states to pick cotton, but these laborers soon moved back west or into nearby towns to run stores and restaurants.

The Japanese Americans were confused by the severe segregation in Mississippi. "When we went into town," said one GI, "we saw the signs in various places for 'Colored' and 'White.' Naturally we were not white, so we would go into the entrance marked 'Colored.' The Caucasians would tell us we were not considered colored so it was all right to use the 'White' entrance." While these soldiers were permitted to use white restrooms and water fountains, they were too foreign-looking for the local white girls, who refused to talk to Nisei GIs.

After a few weeks of living and training together, kotonks and butaheads grew closer. Like brothers, they still argued and fought among themselves yet were quick to unite against any GI who called them Japs or other disrespectful names. The white soldiers quickly learned the "Japs" were ready and capable fighters, especially the ones trained in martial arts.

Camp Shelby's commanders began to see signs that the Nisei were exceptional soldiers. Drill sergeants led the recruits, each man carrying a fifty-pound backpack, on exhausting twenty-five-mile hikes. They were supposed to finish within six hours. It was not unusual for men in other units to fall behind and not finish. But everyone in the Nisei battalion completed the hikes in under six hours. If one man began to lag behind, his buddies would carry the tired soldier's pack or rifle. Sometimes they even carried the soldier himself.

One GI explained this remarkable all-for-one and one-for-all attitude: The men believed that "you can die, but don't embarrass yourself, your buddies, or your family."

The armed forces at the beginning of World War II were segregated, so white, African American, and Japanese American soldiers were usually assigned to separate units. And white officers commanded most black and Nisei companies. But there were some exceptions. The commander of the 232nd Combat Engineer Company was Captain Pershing Hakada, and his five assistants were all Nisei lieutenants. And in another company, one officer was neither Caucasian nor Nisei but of Korean heritage. He was Lieutenant Young Oak Kim. Many Koreans hated the Japanese because Japan had invaded Korea and treated its people brutally. But Kim seemed free of prejudice.

Kim's parents in Los Angeles owned a small grocery store near Little Tokyo. Kim had attended Los Angeles High School, where the students were Chinese, Japanese, Mexican, Jewish, and Italian from surrounding immigrant neighborhoods.

The young man tried to enlist in the Army in 1940, but the recruiter turned him down because of his race. A few months later Kim was drafted. The city boy had never before fired a gun, but he proved to be an excellent marksman. Because of his skill with a rifle, Kim assumed he would be assigned to the infantry. A blunt officer told him otherwise. "Wake up. You've got the wrong shape eyes. You've got the wrong skin. Everything is wrong. You can't be a soldier. People like you aren't soldiers."

The officer assigned Kim to mechanics school to learn to repair trucks and jeeps. Kim's intelligence and hard work impressed the school's commander, who sent the young man to Officer Candidate

School. He graduated at the top of his class, and the Army assigned him to the Japanese American battalion at Camp Shelby.

The Hawaiians did not like the new lieutenant. The butaheads spoke rapidly in their pidgin dialect so he would not be able to understand what they were saying. They mocked his seriousness by calling him GI Kim. His commanders offered to transfer him to another unit, but Kim chose to remain with the Japanese Americans.

Kim and other Nisei GIs frequently visited the WRA camps in Arkansas. On the Fourth of July, 1943, eight hundred soldiers rode chartered buses across the Mississippi River to Camp Jerome to picnic, play baseball, and listen to patriotic speeches. "After seeing the hard-

Nisei soldiers often visited family and friends in the internment camps.
NATIONAL ARCHIVES

ship that the mainland boys' parents were enduring," one butahead recalled, "we became a much closer unit before we went overseas."

Some soldiers, knowing they might not return from the European battlefields, traveled out west to see their families. Shig Doi described his visit to the WRA camp in Colorado:

"I think I only spent two or three days at Amache because it was so depressing that I couldn't stay anymore. My mom was trying to do her best to keep me happy. The day that I was supposed to leave she wanted to make me something, but she couldn't fix anything for me. There wasn't anything. She felt really bad about not having anything for me. . . . When I got on the train one Caucasian guy asked me, 'What kind of camp is that?' I just couldn't tell him what the hell it was. So I kept my mouth shut."

Toward the end of basic training, the Nisei battalion lost some of its smartest soldiers to a top-secret assignment. The men had volunteered for Military Intelligence School. Their missions would not be revealed until after the war.

In August 1943, the Army shipped the Hawaiian 100th overseas. The 442nd would follow nine months later. Camp Shelby had trained the Nisei soldiers for war, but no amount of training could prepare them for the hardships and horrors they would endure on the battlefields of Italy and France.

5

The Purple Heart Battalion

T HE ABBEY OF MONTE CASSINO sat like a small crown high on top of Monte Cassino. Military experts said the Benedictine abbey was the strongest fortress in the world. But the warring armies had promised not to occupy the stone building because it was one of Europe's most religious sites. The Allies—a coalition of armies led by the United States and Great Britain—believed the Germans had broken their promise.

Monte Cassino was flanked on the west by the Liri River Valley and on the east by the Rápido River Valley. From across these valleys, the sides of the seventeen-hundred-foot mountain looked nearly vertical. The abbey perched on top of the mountain faced south, overlooking the broad plain where the two valleys converged, like a big V. It was here that Highway 6, the main route through the steep mountains surrounding Cassino, crossed the Rápido River and proceeded northwest through the Liri Valley. When the Allied armies ventured onto the plain, enemy artillery shells rained down on them with uncanny accuracy. The soldiers below suspected the Germans were using the abbey as an observation post from which they could direct their deadly artillery fire.

The Allies had invaded the Italian mainland in early September 1943 and were fighting their way up Highway 6. They had to capture the abbey before they could continue north to their prize objective, Rome, the Italian capital. The battle for Monte Cassino was one of the war's most horrific fights. It was where the Nisei unit earned the nickname "the Purple Heart Battalion." The Purple Heart is a medal that the Army awards soldiers wounded in combat.

The 100th Infantry Battalion landed in Italy just two weeks after Allied forces had invaded the Italian mainland. These forces included soldiers from many different countries—Brazil, India, Australia, New Zealand, Canada, and Poland. The United States and Great Britain—England, Ireland, Scotland—provided the largest number of soldiers. The thirteen hundred Japanese Americans joined tens of thousands of GIs of the U.S. Fifth Army under the command of General Mark Clark.

The GIs knew little about the land they had invaded. They did know Italy was a small country that looked very different from the United States. The boot-shaped peninsula is eight hundred miles long and less than a hundred miles wide. Everything—from the stone houses to the gnarled grapevines and the squat olive trees—seemed old. Even Highway 6 was old. It had once been the Via Casilina, the road Roman legions had marched along to stop Hannibal's invasion two thousand years earlier.

The Americans had imagined Italy to be a sunny country, but the autumn and winter of 1943 were among the worst ever. It rained nearly every day in October, and the temperatures were unusually cold. The men still wore their summer uniforms. Supplies of warm clothing,

General Mark Clark, the commander of American forces in Italy, reviews the men of the 100th. Nisei soldiers were smaller than Caucasian GIs.
NATIONAL ARCHIVES

food, and even ammunition were slow to reach the front. Rumors circulated that the soldiers were being shortchanged because the Allies were stockpiling supplies in England for a big invasion of German-occupied France.

American troops on a road in Italy. NATIONAL ARCHIVES

The GIs were unprepared for the carnage of war. "In combat you see horrible, horrible things," recalled Young Oak Kim. "People don't die real nice and pretty like in Hollywood pictures. They're mangled horribly." Many soldiers became sick the first time they saw dead Italian civilians and German soldiers lying beside the road. The rotting bodies, often missing heads, arms, or legs, smelled so strong that the men gagged and vomited. But they soon grew used to the sight of corpses.

"I remember one night, it sounds gruesome, but it's true," a GI said, describing his hardened feelings. "The fighting slowed down that one evening. I sat down. We were trying to count heads and a sergeant came up and sat down. I sat on a helmet. He sat on one of the enemy dead. Now, that's terrible. But there, in combat, we didn't give a damn. We were tired. The enemy was stiff, you know. We figured he was out of it. Well, whatever it was, it was over for him, so we sat on him. I started eating my K ration and he [the sergeant] started eating his K ration. You reach a certain low point of sensitivity, you just don't give a damn. This was war. This was terrible. You're fighting so damn hard and you just keep going, and small things don't bother you after a while—like dead bodies."

The first butahead died within days of arriving in Italy. Shigeo "Joe" Takata had volunteered to lead a band of men to knock out an enemy machine gun firing on his company. While they were advancing on the machine-gun nest, an artillery shell exploded nearby and shrapnel hit the sergeant in the head, instantly killing him. The Army awarded Takata a Distinguished Service Cross because he had bravely volunteered to lead the dangerous mission. It was the first of many medals the Nisei would earn by their bravery and their blood.

The Japanese Americans quickly established a reputation as exceptional fighters. Stories about their battlefield feats began to circulate among the other soldiers. One story about the 100th's "two-man army" was particularly popular. Attacked by forty Nazi soldiers armed with machine guns and grenades, Lieutenant Allan Ohata and Private Mikio Hasemoto faced the charge standing side by side, their carbines blazing. They killed thirty-eight of the enemy and captured two. Before the smoke had cleared, fourteen more Germans attacked. The two Nisei killed four and wounded three of the attackers before the remaining Nazis retreated. The pair even managed to repulse a third attack, but soon afterward an artillery shell killed Private Hasemoto.

General Clark said the Nisei were "the best goddamn fighters in the U.S. Army." The 100th's growing reputation earned it the hardest assignments. One of the toughest was to capture the abbey on top of Monte Cassino.

Few soldiers who looked up at the yellow stone building from the

Nisei soldiers inspect a destroyed German vehicle. NATIONAL ARCHIVES

valley below knew why it was so famous. Saint Benedict had established the monastery and the Benedictine order on Monte Cassino fifteen hundred years earlier. Marauders and earthquakes destroyed the first building. The current structure, which was five hundred years old, was built to withstand assaults by both man and nature. The rectangular building was four stories high and the length of two football fields. Behind the thick stone walls, the Benedictine monks preserved priceless treasures of western civilization. The library contained many rare books, including Latin manuscripts by Ovid and Virgil. Artisans had

The Benedictine abbey on top of Monte Cassino. The town of Cassino is at the bottom of the mountain. NATIONAL ARCHIVES

adorned the chapels and crypts with beautiful tapestries, frescoes, and mosaics.

Now the abbey was becoming famous for another reason. It was proving to be the enemy's toughest defense against the Allied invasion of Italy. So many men had died or been wounded on the plain beneath Monte Cassino that GIs nicknamed it "Purple Heart Valley." One group suffered an especially severe beating there.

The 36th "Texas" Division tried to cross the Rápido River in boats, but German artillery and gunfire cut the men down before they reached the opposite bank. Next, the soldiers laid portable Bailey bridges across the river. When the GIs began crossing the metal foot-bridges, they were hit by withering machine-gun fire. Several hundred soldiers managed to reach the north side of the river before German artillery destroyed the bridges and trapped the Americans.

Their buddies on the south side of the Rápido listened anxiously to the gunfire across the river. These soldiers knew German machine guns made a *brrrp* sound, while American guns made a *rat-tat-tat* sound. They heard fewer and fewer American guns until, finally, there was only silence.

The Germans asked for a truce so both sides could remove their casualties. The Nazis even helped American medics locate wounded GIs. The truce was scheduled for only two hours, but it lasted longer, each side reluctant to resume fighting. Over sixteen hundred GIs had been killed or captured in this disastrous attempt to cross the Rápido.

On Monte Cassino, overlooking the river, the Germans were well prepared to stop the invaders. Their engineers had dug into the steep sides of the mountain to build concrete-and-steel bunkers for machine guns and artillery. Nazi soldiers lived in underground quarters connected by passageways. These underground fortifications were difficult for either Allied artillery or airplanes to destroy. The Germans buried thousands of land mines along roads and footpaths, anywhere a vehicle or man might go. One type of mine was called Bouncing Betty. When it was tripped, the mine sprang into the air, exploded, and spewed deadly shards of metal everywhere. At the bottom of the mountain, German engineers dammed the Rápido River, flooding nearby fields. Nazi soldiers chopped down bushes and trees that could have hidden approaching troops, but they left the tree stumps in place to stop any advancing tanks.

The Nisei battalion first attacked Monte Cassino shortly after midnight on January 24, 1944. It was bitterly cold, but few of the men thought about the weather. Howitzers, a type of small cannon, located behind Allied lines fired shells at the German gun positions on the side of the steep mountain. Nazi artillery returned the fire. The shells soaring overhead sounded like freight trains, growing louder and louder until they slammed into the earth with mighty explosions.

The GIs especially hated the "screaming meemies." These were German artillery shells that made an eerie, high-pitched whistle as they sailed through the air. The shells exploded into jagged pieces of iron that could tear a man's head off.

"The air was filled with sound as if every German gun in the valley had fired toward us at the same time," recounted one of the Americans in that attack. "We pushed down as far as we could in terror, and the ground all around us shook with gigantic explosions. The air was full of flying dirt and shrapnel. There was the frightening smell of gunpowder and crash after crash. I did not have time to wonder what was happening to my men. In such a shelling as this each man is isolated from everyone else. Death is immediately in front of him. He only knows that his legs and arms are still there and that he has not been hit yet; in the next instant he might be."

The soldiers who led the advance that night crawled slowly

through the cold water, searching carefully for mines and marking their path with stakes and strips of white tape for other infantrymen to follow. The Germans fired flares into the sky so their gunners could see the Americans in the field below. These phosphorous torches looked like big Fourth of July sparklers as they floated down to earth, casting brilliant white light over the battlefield.

It took all night for the soldiers to pick their way across the muddy, mine-dotted field. After the men reached the protection of a fourteen-foot-high flood wall along the river, they waited for reinforcements to bring ladders so they could scale the wall.

Just as night was fading to morning, two hundred GIs began sloshing across the muddy fields. The American artillery fired canisters that created an artificial smoke screen to obscure them from enemy gunners. But a breeze blew the smoke away. The Germans then unleashed a storm of machine-gun, mortar, and artillery fire on the exposed GIs. Only fourteen men managed to reach the flood wall. Others scurried back to safety, but most were wounded or killed. For the rest of the day, the wounded had to lie in the icy water. It wasn't until dark that medics could safely rescue survivors.

It would have been disastrous for the Nisei to try to cross the river, so the Allied commanders called off the attack. Many of the men were sick with diarrhea, trench foot, and pneumonia from exposure to the winter cold. The GIs withdrew behind the front line to the town of San Michele. There they bathed, changed into clean clothing, and chatted with American Red Cross women, whom soldiers affectionately called Doughnut Dollies. After two days the 100th returned to battle.

Other Allied units already had crossed the Rápido River and surrounded the town of Cassino. The Fifth Army's commanders sent the Japanese Americans up the mountain to capture the abbey. Two companies fought their way to within fifty yards of the Nazis, who were entrenched near the abbey's old walls. There they were stopped by heavy machine-gun fire. The Americans spent the night lying on the cold ground, worrying that the enemy, only one hundred fifty feet away, would attack at daybreak.

The next morning, a German tank rolled toward them. Private Masso "Tankbuster" Awakuni aimed his bazooka at the tank and quickly fired three rounds. The first two shells exploded harmlessly against the steel hull. The third ignited the gas tank, which exploded and engulfed the vehicle in flames, burning the crew alive. All this time the Germans were shooting at Awakuni. One bullet wounded him in the arm. He crawled behind a rock and hid for ten hours until dark, when he rejoined his buddies.

Three medics, who later were honored with Silver Stars for their bravery, cared for the wounded. The constant gunfire kept them from carrying anyone down the hill. One of the wounded men was Major James Lovell. It was the second time since his arrival in Italy four months earlier that the major had been shot. This time Lovell was hit in the leg and in the chest. He fell into a gully. His men tried to reach him, but they were stopped by a hail of enemy gunfire.

Sergeant Gary Hisaoka started digging a trench to the major sixty feet away. After two hours of shoveling in the rocky soil, he had dug only halfway. Frustrated, Hisaoka tossed aside his spade and, ignoring the bullets, darted over to the major. The sergeant was too small to carry the larger man, so he grabbed Lovell's arms and dragged him back to the trench. The Army awarded Hisaoka the prestigious Oak Leaf Cluster to add to the Silver Star he had won earlier. Sergeant Hisaoka was later killed in battle.

Company B of the 100th battalion attacked the heavily fortified town of Cassino at the bottom of the mountain. After fierce house-to-house and even room-to-room fighting, the Nisei captured part of the town. Too many men had been killed or wounded for that small victory, and the commanders ordered Company B to withdraw.

After nearly two months of trying to take the abbey with ground troops, the Allies decided to call in the Army Air Force. A Piper Cub flew over the abbey, dropping leaflets warning people inside that it would be bombed on February 16. In the mountaintop sanctuary, a thousand people, both monks and Italians from the town of Cassino, hid from the war raging around them. The abbot, the elder monk in charge of the abbey, planned to evacuate the building early that morning. But bad weather was forecast for the sixteenth, so the Air Force began bombing a day early. On the morning of the fifteenth, 255 planes dropped over 500 tons of bombs on the abbey and on the town of Cassino. "It was a terrible sight," said Captain Sakae Takahashi, "an awesome sight."

It was at the time the biggest bombing raid in history. The bombs killed three hundred people in the abbey, but hundreds more survived in the building's deep underground rooms. Before the bombing, German soldiers had helped the monks move the precious art and manuscripts to a distant monastery. The monks later said the Germans had never used the abbey for an observation post or for any other military purpose.

After the Air Force had destroyed the old building, the Nazis moved artillery, machine guns, and troops into the stone rubble, which provided excellent protection from the Allied attacks that followed. It took three more months, hundreds of tons of additional bombs, and many more deaths before Polish troops finally captured the abbey on May 18.

Months of heavy fighting reduced the abbey and the town to rubble.
NATIONAL ARCHIVES

Soldiers grimly began referring to the 100th as the Purple Heart
Battalion because of the heavy casualties its men suffered trying to capture the abbey. Over half of the thirteen hundred Nisei who had landed
in Italy four months earlier had been wounded or killed. During that
time, other Japanese Americans from Camp Shelby replaced the casualties. The entire 442nd Regimental Combat Team, some three thou-

sand men, arrived in Italy in the spring of 1944. The Japanese Americans were joined into a single battalion called the 100th/442nd. Rather than abolishing the 100th altogether, the Army commanders decided on this unusual dual designation as a way of honoring the Hawaiian battalion's bravery.

Soon after the 442nd landed in Italy in early June, the Allies marched victoriously into Rome. Yet the world's attention was not on Italy but on the D-Day drama of 4,000 ships carrying 100,000 soldiers across the English Channel to storm the Normandy beaches of German-occupied France. The Normandy invasion began a summer of fierce fighting that grew worse as the Allies neared the German border. By year's end they hoped to invade Germany. The Allies needed their best soldiers for that invasion, so they called the 100th/442nd to France. Back in the United States, people in the WRA camps were on the move, too.

6

Resettlement

"THE 442ND COMBAT REGIMENT was famous now, full of heroes fighting in Europe to help the Allies win the war, and showing that Niseis too could be patriots," observed Jeanne Wakatsuki at Manzanar as she watched her brother Woody board a bus that would take the newly drafted man to an Army training base. "Woody was that kind of Nisei, anxious to prove to the world his loyalty, his manhood, something about his family honor."

By the spring of 1944, nearly one third of the Issei and Nisei had left their camps. They were allowed to move anywhere in the United States except to the West Coast, where there was still a lot of hatred for people of Japanese heritage.

Reports of battlefield atrocities from the Pacific war caused some of the hatred. Hundreds of American prisoners of war died of starvation and cruelty during a notorious incident known as the Bataan Death March. And in Tokyo, captured American airmen were publicly beheaded. These incidents inspired other stories that were probably not true. A missionary in China claimed to have seen Japanese soldiers cut out the heart and liver of a Chinese person and eat them.

Nisei and Issei men began leaving the camps soon after they arrived in 1942. Because of a shortage of agricultural workers, the WRA allowed eight thousand volunteers to move from the camps to sugar-beet farms in Utah, Idaho, Wyoming, and Montana. There they harvested over eight thousand acres, thus saving the valuable sugar-beet crop. The harvest was turned into nearly a million pounds of sugar, which helped feed soldiers fighting the war.

College students also left the WRA facilities. Teachers in California had organized the Student Relocation Committee to find new schools for their former students. By 1944, some four thousand Nisei men and women were enrolled in colleges in the East.

Hundreds of young men, like Woody, left the camps for the Army. After the first volunteers proved to be excellent soldiers, the War

Sergeant Ben Kuroki is surrounded by young autograph seekers on his visit to Heart Mountain. Sergeant Kuroki, a native of Kansas, was one of the few Nisei in the Army Air Force. NATIONAL ARCHIVES

*Several hundred Nisei women
also joined the Army.*
NATIONAL ARCHIVES

Each camp proudly displayed the names of former residents serving in the military.
NATIONAL ARCHIVES

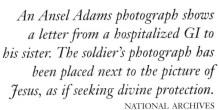

*Mothers with children in the
service hung gold stars in their
windows. Each star represented
a son in uniform.*
NATIONAL ARCHIVES

*An Ansel Adams photograph shows
a letter from a hospitalized GI to
his sister. The soldier's photograph has
been placed next to the picture of
Jesus, as if seeking divine protection.*
NATIONAL ARCHIVES

Department in January 1944 reinstated the draft for nearly twenty
thousand military-age Nisei men. About three hundred of them
refused to register. These men objected to being drafted after having
been deprived of their rights as citizens. Some were classified as con-
scientious objectors, while others were convicted of draft evasion and
imprisoned. But the majority of Nisei registered with their local selec-
tive service boards.

Many more people began leaving the internment camps in 1944

after authority for the WRA facilities was transferred to the Department of the Interior. The head of that department, Harold Ickes, wanted to close all the camps. His department encouraged thousands of people to relocate to Midwestern and East Coast cities, including Cincinnati, St. Louis, Chicago, New York, and Philadelphia. More than 2,600 ethnic Japanese went to Seabrook Farms in southern New Jersey, where they worked in a frozen-food plant. Everyone who left the camps had to pass a security check. Then WRA officials gave them each a twenty-five-dollar relocation allowance, plus three dollars a day for travel expenses.

"Young people are going out of here by the hundreds—into the Army, back east, and to the farms. This will be a very quiet place in a few months," observed a man at Heart Mountain. By mid-1944, over thirty thousand people had left the camps. That spring, authorities closed Camp Jerome in Arkansas and moved its remaining residents to other camps.

In December 1944, the United States Supreme Court ruled that the forced internment violated constitutional principles. That decision meant all the camps had to be closed. Many Japanese Americans left immediately. Jubilant families departed from Amache, Heart Mountain, and Poston, flying streamers, banners, and American flags from the windows of the trains carrying them back home.

But even after the Supreme Court decision, thousands of people remained in the camps, some for as long as sixteen months afterward. They stayed because they had no homes or jobs to return to. Or because they were scared of the anti-Japanese hatred that still existed in the Pacific states.

A California state senator proposed barring all people of Japanese heritage from the state. The proposal was withdrawn only after another

This young woman left Topaz to attend college in New York City.
NATIONAL ARCHIVES

senator introduced six veterans of the 100th/442nd on the state senate floor. Two of the veterans walked with crutches and a third had lost a leg.

Fletcher Bowron, the mayor of Los Angeles, where the nation's largest number of ethnic Japanese had once lived, said he did not want the Issei or Nisei returning to his city. The mayor also said the Nisei should be stripped of their citizenship and all people of Japanese heritage should be sent back to Japan.

Ansel Adams, one of America's most famous photographers, in 1944 published *Born Free and Equal,* a book of text and photographs praising Manzanar's residents. Caucasians violently objected to the favorable portrayal and burned the books.

The hostility was worse in small towns. One store displayed a sign that read, NO CIGARETTES. NO NEGROES. NO JAPS. Some of the violence was quite peculiar. Someone burned a family's laundry as it hung drying in their backyard.

The American Legion in Hood River, Oregon, removed the names of sixteen Nisei soldiers from the town's war memorial. And the local newspaper published names of five hundred residents who did not want Issei or Nisei living in Hood River. Most of the violence occurred in rural farming communities. Some observers believe it was inspired mainly by people who were afraid of economic competition from hard-working Japanese farmers.

Nisei soldiers fighting in Europe received letters from their families describing the problems back home. Shig Doi, one of the men who

A family leaving Heart Mountain for a new home in the East shows their pass to the guard. NATIONAL ARCHIVES

had volunteered for the 442nd, explained how his family was treated when they first returned from Amache to their farm in Placer County northeast of Sacramento. Someone tried to "dynamite our packing shed, but somehow the fuse didn't go off. So second, they were going to burn it down. Well, there's always good in some people, and one of the fruit managers told my brother, 'Watch out, they're going to burn your shed down tonight.' So my brother had the firehose ready, and the minute he saw some flame he was able to put it out. Then the following night they fired a shotgun through our house.

"See, I was getting shot at from the enemy, and then at home in my own country, people were shooting at my dad. I was risking my life for this country, and my government was not protecting my folks." At the time that his parents were having trouble in Placer County, California, Doi and the 100th/442nd were in France, engaged in one of their most difficult battles.

7

Rescuing the Lost Battalion

THE 100TH/442ND arrived in the French port of Marseilles at the end of September 1944. In the four months following the D-Day invasion, the Allied armies had pushed the German army across France. They liberated the nation's capital, Paris, in August and then forced the enemy north into the Vosges Mountains separating France and Germany. The Nazis took a stand in those mountains, determined to stop the Allies from invading their country.

Allied commanders assigned the three thousand Japanese Americans to the 36th Division of the Seventh Army, under the command of Major General John E. Dahlquist. The general immediately sent these fresh troops into battle.

The first Nisei to die in France was Staff Sergeant Tomosu Hirata. He was killed while freeing Biffontaine, a village east of Bruyères, from Nazi occupation. The Army usually shipped dead soldiers home to the United States or buried them in special cemeteries in France. But Biffontaine's residents wanted to express their gratitude to the men who had freed them. They asked Hirata's parents to leave their son in the village's cemetery and promised to care for his grave forever.

Nisei soldiers in France walk past the ruins of a German half-track.
NATIONAL ARCHIVES

Troops marching through the Vosges Mountains. NATIONAL ARCHIVES

Another casualty in the battle for Biffontaine was Young Oak Kim. "I started to go into shock. An ice-cold feeling came in my toes and came up my body," Kim described the feeling after he had been shot. "I thought at any moment I was going to die. I just knew that if it kept creeping, I was dead. . . . Chaplain Yosh was there praying and crying and asking me to fight. . . . Then all of a sudden for some unknown reason, the creeping . . . suddenly stopped, and then started to recede." Medics evacuated Kim to a military hospital where he recovered from his wound.

Two weeks after Biffontaine, for the first time since the Nisei's arrival in France, General Dahlquist sent the 100th/442nd behind the lines for a much-needed rest. Fourteen days and nights of continual fighting had exhausted the soldiers. The weary men showered and dressed in clean uniforms. They were looking forward to sleeping in warm cots without worrying about being blown to smithereens by enemy artillery. Then they received an urgent radio message. Be ready by daybreak, General Dahlquist ordered, to rescue a trapped battalion.

An estimated 700 Nazis had surrounded 275 Americans from the First Battalion of the 141st Regiment, 36th Division. It was part of the same "Texas" division that had suffered such terrible losses crossing the Rápido River at Monte Cassino. These GIs had been dubbed "the Lost Battalion," although everyone, especially the Germans, knew exactly where they were. The men were on top of a ridge, three miles from the nearest friendly soldier. The Americans were lost in the sense that they were doomed. Everyone expected them to be killed or captured.

"Out of food and water and critically low on ammunition," the Lost Battalion's captain reported in a radio message. "Medical supplies next to nothing; wounded need attention. No way to evacuate them."

The Americans tried to send supplies to their trapped colleagues. Artillery crews shot hollow cannon shells filled with chocolate bars and canteens of water toward the ridge. Some shells missed their target altogether, and others were lost in the dense forest. Airplanes flew overhead and dropped big boxes filled with rations. The boxes were attached to parachutes, and many of them were caught in the branches of tall pines or the wind blew them into the hands of nearby Germans.

Fifty-three of the trapped men volunteered to try to fight their way back to their own lines. Soon after the soldiers walked off the ridge and disappeared into the forest, they ran into the enemy. There was a furious gun battle. Only five men escaped. They returned to the ridge and to the other Americans, who were waiting to be rescued or be captured or die.

At 4 A.M. on October 27, the Nisei set out to rescue the Lost Battalion. At that hour it was so dark in the pine forest that each soldier, walking in single file, had to hold on to the man in front of him to keep from wandering off the trail.

The Japanese Americans knew that they had to reach the trapped GIs quickly, but each step had to be taken cautiously. The enemy had snipers and machine-gun nests hidden everywhere in the forest. The whistle of approaching artillery shells often sent the Americans diving for cover. A soldier described the bizarre scene after one artillery barrage:

"We await the onslaught of powder and steel. . . . Then the slaughter begins. After the barrage, there is silence, an eerie kind of silence. . . . As expected, many are wounded seriously, a few are buried in their slit trenches. A grotesque sight catches my eyes. A shattered hand and arm is embedded on a shattered branch halfway up a tall pine tree and

Left: *A soldier in his foxhole carefully watches for the enemy, who is only a few hundred feet away.* NATIONAL ARCHIVES

Right: *Medics carrying one of the many wounded Nisei to an aid station.* NATIONAL ARCHIVES

it's waving at me. It sends chills up my spine and makes me want to vomit. Our worst imaginations when we first entered the Vosges forests have come true. Trees with human parts."

The temperature was below freezing and cold rain fell steadily. A ghostly fog swirled through the evergreen forest. "You couldn't see the enemy as you moved from cover to cover," said one GI. "You found out where the enemy was only after being shot at."

On their second day, snow began to fall as the Nisei fought their way to within a half mile of the Lost Battalion. General Dahlquist came forward to check on their progress. The general suspected the Nazis were bringing in reinforcements, so he ordered the Nisei to break through to the Lost Battalion at all costs. The battle grew fiercer.

"The firefight was almost continuous every day," said one soldier. "They had the 'Lost Battalion' really surrounded, and my platoon was cut down. We lost our platoon leader, next our platoon sergeant, then our squad leader. Finally the assistant squad leader. . . . Actually our fighting was like Indian fighting. You never knew if the enemy is going to be ten feet, or fifty feet [away], or if he's going to be right behind you."

The Nisei advanced slowly. Then, impatient with his men's slow progress, Colonel Alfred A. Pursall stood up, drew his pair of pearl-handled .45s from their holsters, and called for his troops in Company I and Company K to charge up the hill with him.

Artillerymen, radiomen, and other soldiers who did not normally join frontline charges joined in. "I'm an artilleryman," Francis Tsuzuki remembered thinking. "I don't have to charge, but like a damn fool, I charged up the hill."

Private First Class Jim Y. Tazio, a radio operator with a bulky twenty-five-pound radio strapped to his back, also joined the charge. He kept the crew of an enemy machine-gun nest distracted while other GIs destroyed the nest with grenades. A bullet wounded Tazio, but he shot two of the enemy before a grenade explosion knocked him out. He awoke and saw his intestines spilling out of a gaping hole in his stomach. Tazio eventually recovered from his wounds and was awarded a Distinguished Service Cross.

As the Nisei advanced, the Germans retreated. They left behind a machine-gun crew to delay the Americans while the other Nazis slipped away. The Nisei quickly killed the enemy gun crew. Suddenly, there was no more shooting. An eerie silence settled over the forest.

Mutt Sakumoto, another radioman, remembered dodging from tree to tree when he saw something move ahead of him. Sakumoto took cover behind a thick pine and radioed headquarters, "We've contacted the enemy." Then he cautiously peeked around the tree trunk and saw a man from the Texas division staring at him. Sakumoto shouted into his radio, "We've contacted the Lost Battalion!"

The trapped soldiers were relieved and happy. "I recognized a GI in the trees ahead and shouting and laughing," Sergeant Edward Guy recalled, "I ran down the slope toward the 442nd trooper."

Another grateful GI said, "The Japanese Americans were the most pleasing sight in the world—this short, dark-skinned kid coming up, wearing an American helmet several sizes too big. . . . Here was a brother of mine coming up to save my life."

The Nisei gave the rescued soldiers water and rations. Then they turned to the grim job of caring for their dead and wounded. The second platoon of Company I had only two men left, and the first platoon had been reduced to twenty men. Every officer in Company K had been wounded or killed.

"The Vosges was the most savage battle that I was ever in," one Nisei said. "You never saw the enemy, or, if you did see him, it was in close combat. And, if you got hit, the chance of survival was less because of the cold. The wounded would go into shock very quickly. I think it was really a mess compared to other battles."

Back home, magazines and newspapers published stories describing the brave and dramatic rescue. The whole nation learned how Japanese American soldiers had saved the Lost Battalion. American

Grim-faced GIs line up for honors soon after their rescue of the Lost Battalion.
NATIONAL ARCHIVES

citizens also learned that two thirds of the 100th/442nd had been wounded or killed during eight weeks of fighting in the Vosges Mountains. These men, suspected of disloyalty only two years earlier, now were American heroes.

The Allied armies continued their drive through the mountains and into Germany. The Nisei 522nd Field Artillery Battalion stayed behind to participate in the invasion, while the rest of the 100th/442nd returned to Italy for a last big battle with the Nazis in that country.

8

War's End

BACK IN ITALY, the Japanese Americans were given another difficult mission. The Allied forces had pushed the Germans into the mountains north of Rome. There, determined to stop the Allies, the Nazis had built a heavily fortified defense known as the Gothic Line, which stretched across the top of the Italian peninsula.

The Nisei were attached to the Ninety-second Infantry Division, an African American combat unit. A half million black GIs served in the Army, but racial prejudice kept most of them out of combat units. They were assigned to supply, construction, and stevedore jobs. The Ninety-second was one of only two African American combat divisions in the entire war.

Allied commanders ordered the Ninety-second Infantry to launch a diversionary attack on Monte Folgorita, near the city of Massa, on the western end of the Gothic Line. The Allies wanted to trick the Nazis into sending their reserve troops to Massa so they could launch their main attack on the middle of the Gothic Line.

The U.S. commanders, who had been trying to capture Monte

Folgorita for five months, knew the 100th/442nd were excellent soldiers. They told the Nisei soldiers to devise their own attack plan and capture the mountain within a week. The Japanese Americans set out after dark on April 5. They wanted to surprise the Germans. The men hiked through a gorge until they came to a cliff one hundred twenty feet high. In the final hours of darkness, the soldiers quietly climbed up the rocky wall. Several men lost their footing and fell. One man died and the others were seriously injured. But none of them uttered a sound so as not to betray their comrades.

The Nisei reached the top of the cliff before daybreak and attacked while the Nazis were eating breakfast. The fight was fierce but brief. Only forty-eight hours after their commander had given them a week to take the ridge, the Japanese Americans had captured Monte Folgorita. They quickly pushed ahead, capturing other mountains and cutting crucial supply lines.

Lieutenant Daniel Inouye led his company in an attack on German positions on Monte Nebbione, near the coastal city La Spezia. Inouye, who later became a U.S. senator from Hawaii, described those last days of fighting in his autobiography, *Journey to Washington*. As his company advanced along a ridge, "three machine guns opened up on us. I can still smell that piece of unyielding ground under my face, and hear the *w-hiss* of the bullets tearing above my helmet."

Lieutenant Inouye crawled to within five yards of the machine guns, pulled a grenade from his belt, and jumped up to throw. He suddenly felt a sharp pain in his side, as though he had been punched. He paused briefly, but he knew he had to quickly get rid of the grenade in his hand. It was going to explode in five seconds.

Opposite: *American troops march into the mountains of northern Italy.* NATIONAL ARCHIVES

Inouye ran toward "that angry sputter of flame at the mouth of the nearest machine gun" and threw his grenade into the bunker. It exploded with a shower of dust and metal. Inouye shot several German soldiers who staggered out of the bunker.

Then the lieutenant "looked down to where my right hand was clutching my stomach. Blood oozed wet between the fingers." He had been hit in the stomach. Despite the pain, Inouye knew he had to destroy the other two bunkers. He threw two grenades into the second bunker before he collapsed from loss of blood.

Inouye's men rushed to help him, but German machine-gun fire forced them to dive for cover. While the Nazis were shooting at the other GIs, the lieutenant crawled toward the enemy bunker to throw his last grenade. Inouye described the dramatic scene that followed.

"As I drew my arm back, all in a flash of light and dark I saw him, that faceless German. . . . One instant he was standing waist-high in the bunker, and the next he was aiming a rifle grenade at my face from a range of ten yards. And even as I cocked my arm to throw, he fired and his rifle grenade smashed into my right elbow and exploded and all but tore my arm off. . . . It dangled there by a few bloody shreds of tissue, my grenade still clutched in a fist that suddenly didn't belong to me anymore."

Lieutenant Inouye managed to toss the grenade with his left hand. It exploded in the German's face. Other Nisei soldiers charged the bunker, quickly killing the rest of the enemy. One German fired a final burst of bullets and several hit Inouye. He fell, rolled down the hill, and lost consciousness.

He soon awoke to a grisly sight. "I saw blood pulsing out of the nearly severed artery [of the arm] in regular little geysers and I made a feeble attempt at putting a tourniquet on it. But there wasn't enough upper arm left to work with, so I just fumbled in that mass of muscle and bone until I found the artery and I pinched it closed."

Several GIs tried to help him, but Inouye ordered them to watch for a German counterattack. Medics carried him back to the hospital, and doctors later amputated his right arm.

Four weeks after the Allies began their assault, they had destroyed the German mountain defenses and captured thousands of enemy soldiers. The Nazis in Italy negotiated a cease-fire for that country on May 2, 1945. Five days later, on May 7, the German nation surrendered.

Nisei soldiers with young German prisoners. NATIONAL ARCHIVES

Although Japan had lost most of its recent battles against the United States, and its air force, navy, and army had been decimated, the little country stubbornly refused to surrender. The war in the Pacific dragged on through the summer.

On August 6, 1945, a lone American B-29 bomber, the *Enola Gay*, flew over the industrial city of Hiroshima and dropped a single atomic bomb, incinerating four square miles of the city and immediately killing eighty thousand civilians. Three days later, the United States dropped a second atomic bomb, this one on the city of Nagasaki, causing similar devastation and death. These were the only two atomic bombs that have ever been used in war. On August 14 the Japanese agreed to end the war, with the official surrender taking place on September 2.

After the Allied victory in Europe and in Japan, the public began to learn more about the role of Japanese American soldiers in World War II.

One unit, the 522nd Field Artillery Battalion, had participated in the invasion of Germany. These artillerymen were among the first Allied soldiers to reach Dachau, one of the infamous concentration camps where the Germans killed millions of Jews, Gypsies, homosexuals, and handicapped people. Some observers called America's WRA facilities concentration camps, but they were nothing like the German camps, which were hellish holes of depravity and death.

Not all Nisei soldiers served in the 100th/442nd. Some six thousand Japanese Americans served in the Military Intelligence Service (MIS). The MIS's director of Japanese-language instruction was John Fujio Aiso. He was the same person who fifteen years earlier had not been permitted to represent his Los Angeles high school in an oratorical contest in Washington, D.C. After high school, Aiso attended

Brown University on a scholarship, graduated summa cum laude, and went to Harvard Law School.

The army drafted the thirty-one-year-old attorney in early 1941 and, as it had with Young Oak Kim, first assigned him to mechanics school. Aiso was soon reassigned to the Military Intelligence Service to teach soldiers to read and speak the complex Japanese language. The first MIS soldiers were recruited in the summer of 1943 from among the Nisei who were training at Camp Shelby. Their assignment was then, and for many years afterward, classified as top-secret. The MIS troops were the eyes and ears of the American forces in the Pacific, translating radio messages and captured enemy documents.

Although some Nisei served in the MIS and in other divisions of the armed services, the majority of the 27,000 Japanese Americans who fought in World War II served in the 100th/442nd. This Nisei battalion compiled a record that was remarkable in many ways. One soldier recalled taking a shower with his buddies and noticing that every man had several scars from bullet or shrapnel wounds. It has been estimated that each soldier in the 100th/442nd who saw combat was wounded an average of three times.

The Nisei battalion was the most highly decorated unit in U.S. military history. The Congressional Medal of Honor, the nation's highest military honor, which few people have ever received, was given posthumously to Private First Class Sadao S. Munemori, a young man whose family was interned at Manzanar. Private Munemori had voluntarily transferred from the MIS to the 100th/442nd. In the final days of the war in northern Italy, Munemori attacked two troublesome machine-gun nests. He destroyed both guns. As soon as Munemori rejoined his company, an enemy grenade hit his helmet and bounced into a foxhole at the feet of two other GIs. The private dived on the

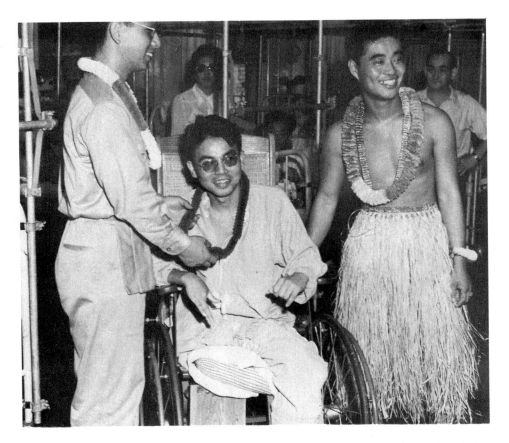

Many soldiers were badly wounded in the war. At this party in a military hospital, the man on the left was blinded in battle. The man in the wheelchair lost an eye, two fingers, and a leg. NATIONAL ARCHIVES

grenade, smothering the explosion with his body. Munemori died saving the two men's lives. More than a half-century later, on June 21, 2000, President Bill Clinton awarded additional Congressional Medals of Honor to Senator Daniel Inouye and nineteen other Nisei World War II veterans.

Other GIs jokingly called the 100th/442nd the Christmas Tree Battalion because its soldiers were so heavily decorated. The Nisei received 9,486 Purple Hearts for their battle wounds. The medals bestowed for heroism now total 21 Congressional Medals of Honor, 52 Distinguished Service Crosses, 560 Silver Stars, and 4,000 Bronze Stars. Twenty-eight men were awarded Silver Stars twice and 1,200 men were awarded Bronze Stars twice. The Nisei record won much praise from prominent Americans.

"You are always thinking of your country before yourselves," said General Mark Clark. "You have never complained through your long periods in the line. You have written a brilliant chapter in the history of the fighting men in America. You are always ready to close with the enemy, and you have always defeated him. The Thirty-fourth Division is proud of you, the Fifth Army is proud of you, and the whole United States is proud of you."

However, when the Nisei soldiers returned home to America, it quickly became apparent that General Clark's feelings were not shared by everyone.

9

Returning Home

THE WAR HAD NOT LEFT AMERICA IN RUINS as it had Japan, France, Italy, Germany, Russia, and—to a much lesser extent—England. But it had been devastating for America's ethnic Japanese. The Issei and Nisei returning home from the WRA camps and from the Army had to rebuild their lives.

People's happiness at coming home turned to dismay when they discovered the destruction to their property. Nobu Miyamoto and his family had operated a prosperous greenhouse and nursery near Seattle. Before they moved to the WRA camp in 1942, they packed their valuables away in trunks and locked up their house securely. The family returned home in 1945 to find their glass greenhouses smashed and the tools that had been stored inside stolen. Thieves had also pried open their trunks to steal jewelry and other valuables. There were many similar stories.

On the Washington coast south of Seattle, a returning fisherman found his oyster beds pirated. The damage was estimated at $100,000. Worse, the fisherman had no income, because the beds would take years to return to health. Farther inland, farm families found the trees in their orchards dying of neglect, fields overgrown, and farm equipment stolen.

In Los Angeles, thieves had broken into the Nichiren Buddhist Church, where six hundred families had stored property. It was "a hopeless mass of destruction," one victim reported, "furniture broken, mirrors smashed to smithereens . . . household goods scattered helter-skelter, trunks broken open, albums, pictures . . . thrown to the four winds. Most things of value, radios, typewriters, sewing machines, Persian rugs have been carried off."

Many families had little to return to. The leases on their businesses

Manzanar residents preparing to return home. LIBRARY OF CONGRESS

Nisei leaving Camp Jerome in Arkansas. NATIONAL ARCHIVES

had lapsed, and their former homes were now occupied by other people. Men and women who had once operated their own farms had to take menial jobs as seasonal laborers picking crops on white people's farms.

"I am doing this kind of work I hadn't done for fifteen to twenty years before evacuation. I used to hire other men to do it for me," one former farm owner explained. "The whole family went out into the orchards and fields when we first came back. . . . The girls kicked at doing farm work. I guess I spoiled them before evacuation. . . . A girl can make more picking fruit and there is no question about her being hired even if she does have slant eyes."

Many of the people released from the camps did not have homes to return to, so they had to live in old Army barracks, hostels, and trailers. NATIONAL ARCHIVES

More than two years after the war, the federal government agreed, under the Japanese American Evacuation Claims Act of 1948, to pay people for their property losses. Many complained the payments were inadequate and continued for decades afterward to press their claims. In 1988, Congress passed House Resolution 442, which was named in honor of the Nisei battalion. This resolution awarded each person who had been interned an apology and $20,000. None of the settlements could replace everything people lost.

One family had owned four thousand acres of rice fields in the San Joaquin Valley as well as a profitable business milling and selling rice.

They had left the business in the care of lawyers, who sold the property and divided up the profits. The owners filed a claim for $1,210,000, but the government paid them less than one third of their claim.

Although this family was able to use its settlement money to start a new company, many Issei were too old to start over. At a time when these people had hoped to be enjoying a comfortable retirement, many of them had lost everything. Their losses not only included homes and jobs; there was emotional and psychological damage as well.

Jeanne Wakatsuki and her family returned to Los Angeles when they left Manzanar in October of 1945. He father's two fishing boats had been repossessed, and the family had very little money. They moved into an apartment in a drab public housing complex. The internment had made Jeanne's father bitter, and he had become an alcoholic. Her mother supported the family by working in a cannery.

For some Issei and Nisei, the internment had been a shameful event, never to be discussed. Alan Nishio, a Sansei, or third-generation Japanese American, first learned his parents had been imprisoned in a WRA camp when he interviewed his mother for a school assignment. "I discovered that my father had owned a grocery store before the war and ended up being a gardener after it and hating it. Before the war he took Mother out once a week to the movies. Since the war, my mother has only seen one movie. Before the war my father didn't drink. But he died two years ago of alcoholism. And I was never really aware of the cause until I started asking about the camp."

Nisei soldiers returning to the West Coast, despite having been hailed as battlefield heroes, met open hostility. Daniel Inouye, who had been promoted to captain, spent two years in an army hospital recovering from the severe wounds he had suffered in Italy. Soon after being released from the hospital, Captain Inouye was in San Francisco, waiting on a ship to sail for Hawaii. He went ashore for a haircut. Inouye described an unpleasant incident at the barbershop.

"'Are you Chinese?' the man said to me. I looked past him at the three empty chairs, the other two barbers watching us closely. 'I'm an American,' I said.

"'Are you Chinese?'

"'I think what you want to know is where my father was born. My father was born in Japan. I'm an American.' Deep in my gut I knew what was coming.

"'Don't give me that American stuff,' he said swiftly. 'You're a Jap and we don't cut Jap hair.'

"I wanted to hit him. I could see myself—it was as though I was standing in front of a mirror. There I stood in full uniform, the new captain's bars bright on my shoulders, four rows of ribbons on my chest, the combat infantry badge, the Distinguished Unit Citations—and a hook where my hand was supposed to be. And he didn't cut Jap hair. To think that I had gone through a war to save his skin—and he didn't cut Jap hair.

"I said, 'I'm sorry for you and the likes of you.' And I went back to my ship."

Unlike the men in the barbershop, there were some Caucasians who were friendly and willing to help the Nisei veterans and their families. The bravery and sacrifices of the 100th/442nd contributed to this change of heart. "The American Japanese won acceptance in large measure through the feats of Nisei soldiers on battlefields abroad," explained one historian. "The all-Nisei combat team was extraordinarily effective as a propaganda weapon. The WRA exploited the success of the 442nd Combat Team to promote the relocation of civilians, first in the East and Middle West and finally on the West Coast."

After people of Japanese heritage were allowed to return to the West Coast, many Caucasians helped with the resettlement. NATIONAL ARCHIVES

Prominent Americans publicly supported the Nisei. General Joseph Stilwell, a hero of the Pacific war, traveled to California to award the Distinguished Service Cross to the family of a GI who had died in combat. Vigilantes had forced the family to leave their rural California home. The general, who was nicknamed "Vinegar Joe" because of his tart outspokenness, made an angry speech.

"The Nisei bought an awful big chunk of America with their blood," Stilwell said at the award ceremony. "I say we soldiers ought to form a pickax club to protect Japanese Americans who fought the war with us. Anytime we see a barfly commando picking on these kids or discriminating against them, we ought to bang him over the head with a pickax. I'm willing to be a charter member. We cannot allow a single injustice to be done to the Nisei without defeating the purposes for which we fought."

Many other Caucasians also helped the homeless men, women, and children. The American Legion, Veterans of Foreign Wars, Society of Friends, and other groups provided housing, furniture, food, and jobs.

The Japanese immigrants had long been accustomed to helping one another, as they had with the *tanomoshi* or cooperative banks, and once again they worked together to make each other's lives as comfortable and secure as possible. In the cities there was a severe housing shortage, caused by people who had migrated from farms and small towns for the high-wage jobs in the war industries and by the millions of veterans suddenly returning to civilian life. Japanese churches organized hostels to provide food and shelter for the people returning from the camps.

Life began to return to the way it had been before the evacuation. "When I came back here in January, it was solid Negroes around here," one former camp resident said, describing the quick transition in Los Angeles's Little Tokyo. "I wondered if this would ever be Japanese town again. Then during the summer and fall, they really started coming back. Soon there were more Japanese than Negroes, and Japanese businesses all up and down the streets. I was surprised." Little Tokyo was again the largest Japanese community in America. And Fletcher Bowron, the mayor of Los Angeles, held a ceremony on the steps of city hall welcoming Issei and Nisei back to the city.

American life changed dramatically after the war. The evacuation in the Pacific states and the horrors of the concentration camps in Europe, where well over six million men, women, and children had been killed, shocked many people. The prejudice that had kept Jews out of neighborhoods, schools, and occupations began to lessen. Black Americans began a sustained movement for civil rights, which eventually broke down the public segregation the Nisei soldiers had seen in Mississippi. And America finally welcomed people of Japanese heritage. The U.S. Congress passed the Walter-McCarran Immigration and Naturalization Act and eliminated race as a bar to naturalization.

Soon after the end of the war, newspapers and magazines that had once printed articles that called people of Japanese heritage hateful names began publishing articles full of praise. *Harper's* magazine called wartime evacuation "Our Worst Wartime Mistake." A sociologist, in an article titled "America's Model Minority," wrote, "By any criterion of good citizenship that we choose, the Japanese Americans are better than any other group in our society, including native-born whites. They have established this remarkable record, moreover, by their own almost totally unaided effort. Every attempt to hamper their progress resulted only in enhancing their determination to succeed. . . . There is no parallel to this success story."

When President Harry S. Truman awarded the 100th/442nd battalion its seventh Presidential Unit Citation in July 1946, he praised the Nisei soldiers with words that could have been addressed to all people of Japanese descent living in America: "You fought, not only the enemy, but prejudice—and you won."

The ethnic Japanese had survived one of the worst periods of racial persecution in America's history thanks to the very thing they had been persecuted for—their heritage. Generations of Japanese parents, as

Togo Tanaka explained, taught their children *shuushin*, the Japanese code of ethics—honor, loyalty, service, and obligation. It was this heritage, these values, that helped families endure life in the WRA camps and helped young men bravely face death on the battlefield.

After the war, it became much easier for the Nisei, and their children, the Sansei, to join the mainstream of American life. Many Japanese American veterans became prominent citizens. John Aiso was appointed to the California Court of Appeals, becoming at the time the highest ranking Nisei jurist on the mainland. When Hawaii became the fiftieth state on August 21, 1959, Daniel K. Inouye was the first Japanese American elected to the U.S. Congress. Three years later, the war hero became the first Japanese American U.S. senator. Bill Hosokawa was a young journalist when he was interned at Heart Mountain, where he started publishing the camp newspaper, the *Heart Mountain Sentinel*. After the war, Hosokawa became an editor at the *Rocky Mountain News* in Denver, Colorado, and the author of several books about Japanese American history.

Today, Japanese Americans are still a small percentage of the American population, but they are involved in all aspects of national life. In the professions, they are business people, soldiers, farmers, politicians, musicians, actors, and astronauts. Despite their success, however, the Issei and Nisei who lived through the mass evacuations and internments of World War II seem incapable of forgetting that experience.

Jeanne Wakatsuki, who grew up to be a journalist and wrote under the name of Jeanne Wakatsuki Houston, describes in her beautifully written book *Farewell to Manzanar* returning to the site of the camp twenty-five years later:

"As I came to understand what Manzanar had meant," she wrote,

Private First Class Masao Masuda with his father, who had recently returned from Gila River. Three of Masuda's brothers served in the Army and one was killed in Italy. NATIONAL ARCHIVES

"it gradually filled me with shame for being a person guilty of something enormous enough to deserve that kind of treatment. In order to please my accusers, I tried, for the first few years after our release, to become someone acceptable. I both succeeded and failed."

Jeanne visited Owens Valley in April 1967. It was the same time of year that she and her family had arrived at Manzanar in 1942. A cold wind blew down from the snowcapped mountains as she walked over the arid ground, searching for remains of the old camp.

She first saw the twelve-foot-high white obelisk that stands near a dozen graves. The black Japanese lettering on the monument reads, A MEMORIAL TO THE DEAD. Pear trees still stood nearby, and she could smell their fragrant spring blossoms. Jeanne next noticed a ring of stones. This was the center of the camp where the flagpole had stood. Each morning a small group of men, a flag-raising detail, had stood at attention with their hands across their hearts as they raised the Stars and Stripes.

Jeanne remembered her family crowded into the two small dusty

The monument at Manzanar. LIBRARY OF CONGRESS

rooms. She thought of her brother boarding a bus that would carry him to an Army camp. Thankfully, unlike many Nisei soldiers, he had returned from the war alive. And she thought of her father and mother, now both dead. Jeanne imagined she heard the voices of the thousands of men, women, and children who had lived here. And she wondered if the evacuation had shaped their lives as it had shaped hers.

"I had nearly outgrown the shame and the guilt and the sense of unworthiness," she wrote in the final chapter of her book. "This visit, this pilgrimage, made comprehensible, finally, the traces that remained and would always remain, like a needle."

The United States of America, through its Constitution and laws, promises equal and fair treatment to all of its people. It had betrayed that promise, and this betrayal can never be completely forgotten by the betrayed.

CHRONOLOGY

1853
Commodore Matthew C. Perry sails into Tokyo Harbor.

1871
Anti-Chinese riot in Los Angeles.

1882
Chinese Exclusion Act: This law keeps Chinese migrants from legally coming to the United States.

1906
San Francisco school board orders the segregation of Japanese American students.

1907
Gentlemen's Agreement between the United States and Japan: Japan voluntarily curtails immigration to the United States.

1913
California Alien Land Law: Noncitizens are not allowed to own property.

1924
Congress passes the Johnson-Reed Act, with provisions for Oriental exclusion.

1939
German troops invade Poland, causing Britain and France to declare war on Germany. It is the beginning of World War II.

1941
The Japanese bomb Pearl Harbor (December 7); the next day the United States enters the war.

1942
January
FBI raid on Terminal Island.

February
President Franklin D. Roosevelt signs Executive Order 9066, establishing restricted areas.

March
President Roosevelt establishes the War Relocation Authority (WRA).

June
The 100th Infantry Battalion arrives at Camp McCoy in Wisconsin.

November
The announcement of the "Application for Leave Clearance" questionnaire causes disturbances at the WRA camps.

1943
January
The 100th moves from Camp McCoy to Camp Shelby.
The War Department announces plan to accept Nisei volunteers for a special combat unit.

February
Nisei from the WRA camps arrive at Camp Shelby.
The 442nd Regimental Combat Team is activated.

September
The 100th arrives in Italy.

1944
January
The three-month battle for Monte Cassino begins.
The draft reinstated for Nisei men.

September
100th/442nd sent to the Vosges Mountains in France.

October
The 100th/442nd rescues the Lost Battalion.

November
Franklin D. Roosevelt wins an unprecedented fourth term as president of the United States.

December
The Supreme Court rules that internment of Japanese Americans violated constitutional protections.

1945
January
Japanese Americans begin returning to West Coast.

April
Franklin D. Roosevelt, who has been president since 1933, dies.
The 100th/442nd breaks the German Gothic Line.

May
Germany surrenders (May 7).

August
An atomic bomb is dropped on Hiroshima (August 6), and a second atomic bomb is dropped on Nagasaki three days later.

September
Japan surrenders.

1946
March
Tule Lake, the last WRA camp, closes.

July
President Harry S. Truman awards the 100th/442nd its seventh Presidential Unit Citation.

1952

The Walter-McCarran Immigration and Naturalization Act repeals the Johnson-Reed Act of 1924 and eliminates race as a bar to naturalization.

1980

Congress establishes the Commission on Wartime Relocation and Internment of Civilians.

1988

A congressional bill awards each Japanese American who was imprisoned $20,000 and an apology. Congress symbolically names the bill House Resolution 442 in honor of the Nisei battalion.

1999

Workers in Washington, D.C. begin constructing a monument to Japanese Americans who were sent to relocation camps and to those who served in World War II. The centerpiece of the $10 million monument near the U.S. Capitol will be two statues of cranes whose wings are tied by barbed wire.

2000

President Bill Clinton awards Congressional Medals of Honor to Senator Daniel Inouye and nineteen other Nisei veterans of the 100th/442nd Regimental Combat Team. The inscription on this medal reads in part, "for conspicuous gallantry and intrepidity at the risk of life, above and beyond the call of duty."

END NOTES

Chapter 1
War Hysteria

The opening quotation is from *The Kikuchi Diary—Chronicle from an American Concentration Camp: The Tanforan Journals of Charles Kikuchi*, John Modell, ed. (Urbana: University of Illinois, 1973). Much of the information on the Japanese American community's reaction to the bombing of Pearl Harbor and the immediate aftermath is drawn from Audrie Girdner and Anne Loftis's *The Great Betrayal: The Evacuation of the Japanese-Americans During World War II* (New York: Macmillan, 1969), Bill Hosokawa's *Nisei: The Quiet Americans* (New York: Morrow, 1969), Page Smith's *Democracy on Trial: The Japanese American Evacuation and Relocation in World War II* (New York: Simon & Schuster, 1995), and Michi Weglyn's *Years of Infamy: The Untold Story of America's Concentration Camps* (New York: Morrow, 1976).

Chapter 2
Asians in America

Two books particularly helpful for this chapter were Roger Daniels's *Asian America: Chinese and Japanese in the United States Since 1850* (Seattle: University of Washington Press, 1988) and Brian Niiya, ed., *Japanese American History: An A–Z Reference from 1868 to the Present* (New York: Facts on File, 1993).

Chapter 3
Barbed Wire Communities

There are many books about individual relocation camps. John Armor's *Manzanar* (New York: Times Books, 1988), with an introduction by novelist John Hersey, is a repackaging of Ansel Adams's photographs of the residents of that relocation camp first published in his book *Born Free and Equal* (New York: U.S. Camera, 1944), which some people burned because of its sympathetic depictions. Details about the whole ten-camp system can be found in

109

Girdner and Loftis's *The Great Betrayal*, Hosokawa's *Nisei*, Smith's *Democracy on Trial*, Weglyn's *Years of Infamy*, and John Tateishi's *And Justice for All: An Oral History of the Japanese American Detention Camps* (New York: Random House, 1984). The permanent exhibit at the Japanese American National Museum in Los Angeles, which includes a partially reconstructed barracks, as well as the thousands of photographs documenting the relocation at the National Archives in Washington, D.C., enhanced my descriptions of the WRA camps.

Chapter 4
Training Camp

Of the numerous books about the 100th and the 442nd, those I found most useful include Masayo Umezawa Duus's *Unlikely Liberators: The Men of the 100th and the 442d* (Honolulu: University of Hawaii Press, 1987), Dorothy Matsuo's *Boyhood to War: History and Anecdotes of the 442nd Regimental Combat Team* (Honolulu: Mutual Publishing, 1972), Thomas D. Murphy's *Ambassadors in Arms: The Story of Hawaii's 100th Battalion* (Honolulu: University of Hawaii Press, 1954), Orville C. Shirey's *Americans: The Story of the 442d Combat Team* (Washington: Infantry Journal, 1947), Chester Tanaka's *Go for Broke: A Pictorial History of the Japanese American 100th Infantry Battalion and the 442nd Regimental Combat Team* (Richmond, Calif.: Go for Broke, Inc., 1982), and Jack K. Wakamatsu's *Silent Warriors: Memoir of America's 442nd Regimental Combat Team* (New York: Vantage, 1995). The oral history collection at the Japanese American National Museum provided several good anecdotes. Especially useful was the oral history of Young Oak Kim, Colonel U.S. Army (ret.), August 28, 1995, by Karen L. Ishizuka and Robert A. Nakamura.

Chapter 5
The Purple Heart Battalion

Christopher Buckley's *Road to Rome* (London: Hodder Stoughton Ltd., 1945) is a well-written description of the Allied drive up the Italian peninsula and the destruction of Monte Cassino. Another description of Monte Cassino is found in Robert Leckie's *Delivered from Evil* (New York: Harper & Row, 1987). Lyn Crost's *Honor by Fire: Japanese Americans at War in Europe and the*

Pacific (Novato, Calif.: Presidio, 1994) is a good source for the 100th/442nd in Italy and France. Additional information is provided by Duus's *Unlikely Liberators*, Shirey's *Americans*, Tanaka's *Go for Broke*, Wakamatsu's *Silent Warriors*, and *The Italian Campaign* (Alexandria, Va.: Time-Life Books, 1978) by Robert Wallace and the editors of Time-Life Books.

Several videos contributed to my understanding of the feats of the Japanese American soldiers. My favorite was *The 442nd: Duty, Honor, and Loyalty* by Video Rights Group, Honolulu. The others that I found interesting were: *Nisei Soldier: Standard Bearer for an Exiled People*, Vox Productions, 1984, 1460 Washington Street, San Francisco, CA 94109; *The Color of Honor: The Japanese American Soldier in World War II*, which is about the Nisei role in the Military Intelligence Service, produced and directed by Loni Ding, 1987, and distributed by National Asian American Telecommunications Association, 346 South Ninth Street, San Francisco, CA 94103; and *Honor Bound—A Personal Journey: The Story of the 100th/442nd Regimental Combat Team, 50 Years Later*, Wendy Hanamura, executive producer and writer, and Joan Saffa, producer and director, available with a teacher's classroom guide from the National Japanese American Historical Society, 1684 Post Street, San Francisco, CA 94115, njahs@njahs.org.

Chapter 6
Resettlement

The problems Japanese Americans faced after leaving the relocation camps are well documented in Girdner and Loftis's *The Great Betrayal*, Hosokawa's *Nisei*, Smith's *Democracy on Trial*, and Weglyn's *Years of Infamy*.

Chapter 7
Rescuing the Lost Battalion

There are numerous descriptions of the rescue of the Lost Battalion, a drama that Americans in 1944 followed in their daily newspapers. The sources I used are Crost's *Honor by Fire*, Duus's *Unlikely Liberators*, Shirey's *Americans*, Franz Steidl's *Lost Battalions: Going for Broke in the Vosges, Autumn 1944* (Novato, Calif.: Presidio, 1997), Tanaka's *Go for Broke*, and Wakamatsu's *Silent Warriors*. Young Oak Kim describes being shot in his oral history at the Japanese American National Museum.

Chapter 8
War's End

Daniel K. Inouye's autobiography, written with Lawrence Elliott, *Journey to Washington* (New York: Prentice Hall, 1967), provides dramatic descriptions of the U.S. senator's military service. I also used Duus's *Unlikely Liberators*, Shirey's *Americans*, Tanaka's *Go for Broke*, Wakamatsu's *Silent Warriors*, and Wallace's *The Italian Campaign*.

Chapter 9
Returning Home

The struggle by Japanese Americans to rebuild their lives after the war is based on information from Girdner and Loftis's *The Great Betrayal*, Hosokawa's *Nisei*, Weglyn's *Years of Infamy*, Inouye's *Journey to Washington*, and Jeanne Wakatsuki Houston and James D. Houston's *Farewell to Manzanar: A True Story of Japanese American Experience During and After World War II Internment* (New York: Bantam, 1995).

OF FURTHER INTEREST

Books

Adams, Ansel, photographs. John Hersey, John Armor, and Peter Wright, text. *Manzanar*. New York: Times Books, 1988.

Bunting, Eve. Chris K. Soentpiet, illustrator. *So Far from the Sea*. New York: Clarion, 1998.

Daniels, Roger. *Asian America: Chinese and Japanese in the United States Since 1850*. Seattle: University of Washington Press, 1988.

Davis, Daniel S. *Behind Barbed Wire: The Imprisonment of Japanese Americans During World War II*. New York: Dutton, 1982.

Girdner, Audrie, and Anne Loftis. *The Great Betrayal: The Evacuation of the Japanese-Americans During World War II*. New York: Macmillan, 1969.

Hosokawa, Bill. *Nisei: The Quiet Americans*. New York: Morrow, 1969.

Houston, Jeanne Wakatsuki, and James D. Houston. *Farewell to Manzanar: A True Story of Japanese American Experience During and After World War II Internment*. New York: Bantam, 1995.

Kitagawa, Daisuke. *Issei and Nisei: The Internment Years*. New York: Seabury, 1967.

Mochizuki, Ken. Dom Lee, illustrator. *Baseball Saved Us*. New York: Lee & Low, 1993.

Niiya, Brian, ed. *Japanese American History: An A–Z Reference from 1868 to the Present*. New York: Facts on File, 1993.

Okubo, Miné. *Citizen 13660*. New York: Columbia University Press, 1946.

Shirey, Orville C. *Americans: The Story of the 442d Combat Team*. Washington: Infantry Journal, 1947.

Sinnott, Susan. *Our Burden of Shame: Japanese-American Internment During World War II*. New York: Franklin Watts, 1995.

Smith, Page. *Democracy on Trial: The Japanese American Evacuation and Relocation in World War II*. New York: Simon & Schuster, 1995.

Steidl, Franz. *Lost Battalions: Going for Broke in the Vosges, Autumn 1944*. Novato, Calif.: Presidio, 1997.

Tanaka, Chester. *Go for Broke: A Pictorial History of the Japanese American 100th Infantry Battalion and the 442nd Regimental Combat Team.* Richmond, Calif.: Go for Broke, Inc., 1982.

Tateishi, John, ed. *And Justice for All: An Oral History of the Japanese American Detention Camps.* New York: Random House, 1984.

Tunnell, Michael O. *The Children of Topaz: The Story of a Japanese-American Internment Camp.* New York: Holiday House, 1996.

Uchida, Yoshiko. *Journey to Topaz.* Berkeley, Calif.: Creative Arts Books, 1985.

Wakamatsu, Jack K. *Silent Warriors: Memoir of America's 442nd Regimental Combat Team.* New York: Vantage, 1995.

Wallace, Robert, and the editors of Time-Life Books. *The Italian Campaign.* Alexandria, Va.: Time-Life Books, 1978.

Video Documentaries

The 442nd: Duty, Honor, and Loyalty. Video Rights Group, Honolulu.

Nisei Soldier: Standard Bearer for an Exiled People. Vox Productions (1460 Washington Street, San Francisco, CA 94109), 1984.

The Color of Honor: The Japanese American Soldier in World War II. Produced and directed by Loni Ding, 1987. Distributor, National Asian American Telecommunications Association, 346 South Ninth Street, San Francisco, CA 94103.

Honor Bound—A Personal Journey: The Story of the 100th/442nd Regimental Combat Team, 50 Years Later. Wendy Hanamura, executive producer and writer. Joan Saffa, producer and director. Available with a teacher's classroom guide from the National Japanese American Historical Society, 1684 Post Street, San Francisco, CA 94115.

Prejudice and Patriotism: The Story of Japanese American Military Service During WWII. Chris Kobayashi and Calvin Roberts.

Yankee Samurai. Belbo Film Productions. Written and directed by Katriel Schory, 1986.

Internet Resources

http://www.nikkeiheritage.org/ National Japanese American Historical Society in San Francisco.

http://www.janm.org/ The Japanese American National Museum in Los Angeles.

INDEX

Page numbers in *italic* type refer to illustrations.

STORAGE